Praise for **thepurplebook**®

"Move over, Yellow Pages!" —*Time*

"A roadmap for shopping the Internet"
—*O Magazine*

"The Bible of Online Shopping Guides"
—*Kirkus Reviews*

"Shopaholics, rejoice! Like the Yellow
Pages—but, well, purple—this book is witty
and comprehensive." —*Boston Herald*

"Think of it as a Google for shoppers....The
sleekly designed book brims with helpful
cross-references and hints for getting the
most out of an online shopping experience."
—*Publishers Weekly*

"A well-planned guidebook, much like the
popular dining directories compiled by
Zagat—only bigger." —*Los Angeles Times*

"A consumer haven." —Bookreporter

thepurplebook®
wedding

the definitive guide
to exceptional
online shopping

WEDDING EDITION

Hillary Mendelsohn

thepurplebook®
wedding edition

Editor-in-chief & Founder
Hillary Mendelsohn

Co-Founder
Lawrence Butler

Author
Ian Anderson

Art Director
Jerome Curchod

Technology Director
Christian Giangreco

Copyright © 2008 by thepurplebook LLC
All rights reserved.

thepurplebook is a registered trademark of thepurplebook LLC

First Edition: January 2008
10 9 8 7 6 5 4 3 2 1

ISBN-10: 0-9799266-0-2
ISBN-13: 978-0-979926-0-0
LCCN: 2007906857

Cover design by Jerome Curchod
Interior design by Jerome Curchod
Printed in Canada

This book is dedicated to Michael - planning our wedding was so special and memorable, and was the inspiration for this book.

*

It is also dedicated to my mom, who lovingly helped plan my dream wedding—we had the best time!!!

*

And to my dad, who paid for it and walked me down the aisle holding my hand tighter than you can imagine, squeezing every ounce of love he could before he gave me away.

acknowledgments

Over the past six years, I have assembled a special group of people that have become my team. Together we have turned a good idea into a great business! I appreciate them all for their individual gifts:

Larry – for your neverending confidence, support and partnership;

Ian – for your exceptional talent, beautifully written words and loyal dedication;

Jerome – for your inspired visual sensibility;

Christian – for your technical prowess.

Jeffrey, you always find a way to help us to make it work.

Larry, I love having you represent **thepurplebook**! You have always been a mentor, confidant and dear friend.

Each of you means the world to me, and I count on your talent, your gifts and most of all your friendship. I am truly grateful to have you all in my world.

thepurplebook®
wedding

CONTENTS

foreword

Ring the bells and pop the corks, **thepurplebook** wedding edition is here. Following the successful release of **thepurplebook** baby and based on the acclaimed annual editions of **thepurplebook: the definitive guide to exceptional online shopping**, we hope you will raise a glass and toast our newest special edition.

Since our inaugural edition in the fall of 2003, online shoppers and retailers have discovered and encouraged our growth. In the meantime, I have been relentlessly scouring the world wide web so every book is fresh and full of new sites.

With this very special edition we vow to provide those of you planning a wedding with the very best the internet has to offer, as well as some tried-and-true advice, tips and ideas.

It is my sincere hope that **thepurplebook** wedding will provide helpful information and a great wealth of opportunities that will help make your wedding everything you have always dreamt, and maybe even exceed your expectations.

Sincerely,

Hillary

Introduction

It's the moment you've dreamt about your entire life: standing beside the person you love more than anything in this world, pledging eternal love and commitment to each other in front of all your family and friends. Everybody's smiling and beautifully dressed, the sun is shining, birds are singing and there could be no more magical a day in all the history of mankind.

Many a little girl imagines what her wedding will be like, but it's only when you grow up that you understand there's a lot of planning, stress and cost that goes into making that dream come true. The pages of this book were designed to minimize the blood, sweat and tears of planning a wedding, whether you aim to keep it small or shoot for the moon, celebrate in the simple splendor of nature or create a most elegant fete. Believe it or not, the internet is a fantastic tool that will make nearly all visions of your ceremony and reception easier to realize. No other generation has had such incredible access to so great a variety of traditional and nontraditional items. From selecting bridal attire and party favors to finding cherished keepsakes and amazing gift registries, we will guide you through the ins and outs of shopping online for the biggest day of your life, and help ensure every detail meets or exceeds your expectations. Because with your wedding, as in life, it's the little things that count.

However, all those little details can quickly add up. Saying yes when the question is popped turns out to be the easiest part of the entire process. That one little word sets off a chain reaction of decisions, compromises and transactions that could conceivably become a full time job. In no time at all the endlessly multiplying list of tasks you create for yourself can prove entirely overwhelming.

We've tried to put some order to the chaos by splitting this chapter into several sections detailing every aspect of the traditional American wedding. We address the fun parts, like picking out dresses and accessories; the complicated stuff, such as formulating a guest list; and tedious things like hiring vendors. Along the way, we offer some sites that may assist you with each step, tips to help keep you sane and checklists to prevent you from missing out on the timeless traditions of matrimony.

Of course, choosing which customs to embrace and which to ignore is part of what makes your event a singular personal expression, and we submit each one as an option for your consideration. Just remember, the most important thing is that you are promising to be with the person you love forever, and celebrating the occasion with the people you both care about. Everything else is just icing on the wedding cake.

Planning
Your Wedding

Preparing for a wedding, keep in mind this will be one of the biggest days in both of your lives. If you do your homework, stay true to your priorities, set boundaries, keep organized and don't sweat the small stuff, you can actually enjoy the planning process.

It's important not to try to take on everything by yourself. Traditionally, the groom is responsible for band, honeymoon and transportation, but these days he can be much more hands on. That's right, ladies, a man can plan a wedding. Not only that, but it can actually be an elegant and stylish affair, allowing him to keep his masculinity and actually gain the admiration and respect of all who attend. Determine early on how involved the groom wants to be in the planning process and figure out which elements are particularly important to him. Even just giving him occasional veto power will keep him feeling involved and thus more willing to help out as needed.

And he's not the only one. Enlisting the help of family and friends will allow those close to you to feel more a part of your special time, with the added benefit that participants on both sides of the aisle can get to know each other better before the big day arrives. That said, there's no doubt whose desires take precedence, especially when it comes to the all-important big details.

Let the adventure begin.

>> The Main Event

The process of throwing a wedding takes the average couple about a year, depending on how big a party you intend to throw and how much you plan to spend. The ceremony itself usually doesn't take very long, and neither does it require many resources, with most of the expense going toward outfitting the bride. It's the reception that typically consumes as much as half of your budget. Between dinner, drinks, entertainment, table settings, venue fees and equipment rentals, costs can quickly add up. As a result, you'll want to spend a lot of time and careful consideration when determining the size and scope of your event.

Bear in mind, a wedding—both the ceremony and the reception—should reflect the personal styles of the bride and groom. Even sticking to the following blueprints, there's plenty of room for you to be original and use your imagination, without having to spend a lot of money. After all, the creative touches are what you and your guests will remember the most, whether it's the music you walk down the aisle to, the decorative theme you choose, the location you pick, or the vows you write, that make it your own.

Where & When

Of course, the first major decision you'll want to make with regard to your big day is exactly when that day will be. Presuming the groom's lingering commitment phobias don't intervene, you'll want to narrow down the time of year that makes the best sense for you. You might have your heart set on a special, meaningful date, or local weather may be a concern. Once you've settled on a general time frame, it's a good idea to consider conflicting happenings that may hinder your guests' ability or willingness to attend, such as holidays, graduations and sporting events. In fact, before committing to any date, you might want to check against prior commitments with close family members and friends. This holds particularly true with destination weddings, where any number of professional or personal obligations can keep important guests from making the journey.

Even if you're not inviting guests halfway around the globe to a beautiful island or mountain retreat, you'll want to take travel into account when selecting your wedding's location. If bride and groom don't share the same hometown, a neutral destination might benefit both families. Factor in family members who may have difficulty traveling, and try to select a place accessible to them. You might need to compromise one part of your dream in order to accommodate another: sharing this day with the people who matter most.

Only when you're convinced all the principals are committed should you set the date, as you will most likely need to put a non-refundable deposit down to hold your venue. Granted, the venue itself might dictate your date. Highly desirable sites often book up to a couple years in advance, and even less popular spaces might not be available at the times you request. While this can greatly complicate matters, you shouldn't let it get you down. Alternate locations for the ceremony or reception may not hold the same cachet, but could prove a blessing in disguise. Ask trusted friends and loved ones for suggestions and, between family properties and called-in favors, you may find yourself with more options than you know what to do with.

When selecting a venue, it's important to know exactly the type of wedding you want to have. Start asking your fiancé questions and make lists of each other's priorities. Do you want a small gathering or a large event? Where would you most like to be married? In a church or a backyard? On a mountainside or in a grand ballroom? Whether you opt for a formal or casual setting, the architecture or natural location may effect how many people will fit comfortably, but will also greatly impact your style. To wit, it's not recommended to wear high heels and a formal gown in a forest, and it's tough to get away with wearing a miniskirt in a cathedral. Choose wisely.

The Ceremony

The type of ceremony you choose will usually depend on your families' cultures and traditions. Obviously, religious ceremonies tend to follow specific rituals, which your minister, priest, rabbi or other ordained officiant will help coordinate. Even secular ceremonies customarily adhere to a standard formula, beginning with the bridal procession, and often incorporating personally selected readings leading up to the exchange of vows and rings. However you choose to go, it really doesn't take much to outdo your average government-office, justice-of-the-peace service.

Regardless of whether you wish to have a religious or secular event, you'll find yourself with some flexibility when it comes to choosing your wedding's style. You may opt. for an ultraformal affair, something quite elaborate that evokes an atmosphere of elegance and grandeur, where the bride wears a long train and the groom dons tails, and the ceremony is followed by dinner served on fine china. Or, you may go for something quite casual, say, with bikinis on the beach and a barbecue reception. Most modern weddings fall somewhere in between: something stylish and semi-formal, where the bride and her entourage dress more to personal preference than rules of etiquette, and a catered reception features select dishes or a buffet dinner, an open bar and dancing.

Although costume and venue set the tone for your ceremony, several other elements contribute to a festive or romantic atmosphere. The first step toward adding a touch of pageantry is to select music to be played for the procession, for both the walk down, and back up the aisle. Classical compositions are most common, and "Here Comes the Bride" would heighten the sense of drama even if said bride was wearing jeans and a t-shirt. However, as with everything else, this is at the discretion of the betrothed couple, and any special music, performed live or played from a recording, is likely to set the mood for all in attendance.

Likewise, your choice of lighting may play an important role. Sunlight, whether through stained-glass windows or in the open air, certainly creates a unique ambiance. However, if you're planning an evening service, or do not wish to gamble with capricious weather patterns, the proper placement of candles cannot help but imbue the proceedings with an animated glow, with the happy side effect that everybody will look especially beautiful in the dancing shadows. Of course, your videographer may take exception to this.

So far as visual decorations go, you may consider bows, ribbons and aisle runners, but rarely will you supersede the brilliance of flowers. Festooning the area with arrangements to match or contrast the bride's bouquet will add splashes of color to everyone's eye line, and having your flower girl toss petals behind her as she marches down the aisle will look as pretty as it does darling. Or, you may choose your flowers with your nose, and subtly fill the air with their graceful, natural scents.

The Reception

Your ceremony is the reason your family and friends will come together to celebrate, but don't kid yourself; the reception is the actual celebration. It's no accident the party you throw to toast your new wedded bliss will take more time to set up, and cost more than the ritual that precedes it. Whereas you design your ceremony for yourself, the reception is a feast you throw for your friends and family. It's a blissful union, and often a reunion, a time for everyone to share unadulterated joy and focus on the positive moments of life.

That said: Two of the things people remember most about a wedding are the food and the music. If they've had a great time, they don't remember the color of the tablecloths. In other words, don't knock yourself out trying to make every tiny detail perfect. Focus instead on offering simple comforts and pleasures for your guests to enjoy. After all, you and your new spouse will be too busy taking pictures and receiving congratulations to make sure everyone is enjoying every minute. Provide an open space, a pleasant meal and some groovy music, and the fun will take care of itself. If you have included children, don't forget to have a kids' table with food appropriate for them. You might also consider having a separate room with games, movies and a baby-sitter. The adults will be thrilled with the time off and may better enjoy the party.

Of course, this especially holds true if you offer plenty to drink, and we're not just talking about soda, juice, water and coffee—although the latter in particular will prove indispensable as the party nears its end. If you are not ethically opposed to serving alcohol, provide champagne for toasting, wine to go with dinner and beer to quench the thirsts of your dancing and feasting guests. Spirits will definitely raise the cost of an open bar, but if you select a signature cocktail you should be able to keep your tab down. You will, however, want to make sure that there are shuttles, taxis or sober drivers willing to make sure all get home safely. Assign a trusted groomsman or usher to engage the guests as they leave to prevent drunk driving.

With regard to toasts, they are but one of the traditional reception activities that will bring the crowd together into a unified party. As long as the toasts don't run too long, or too many, they'll spark bouts of laughter and even a few sentimental tears, and provide an excellent forum to show public appreciation, as well as to celebrate special milestones of guests in attendance, like anniversaries and birthdays.

Other reception activities include cutting the cake, tossing the garter and tossing the bouquet. However, the most anticipated custom may be the first dance. Not only does this give the bride and groom a chance to show off any dancing lessons, natural grace or good-humored tomfoolery, but it signifies the opening of the dance floor. Whether you hire a band, a DJ or simply play a mix from your iPod, the primal human urge to celebrate by dancing is impossible to deny, and you might just be surprised at who among your guests spends the most time gettin' down.

The Budget

Here comes the hard part: paying for everything. It's not the most pleasant reality to face as you plan the happiest day of your life, but it's a necessity that must be addressed early in the planning stages. You're going to have to create a budget.

Tradition states that the bride's family pays for most wedding-related costs, whereas the groom usually covers his own attire, boutonnieres, the officiant's fee, groomsmen gifts, rings and honeymoon. Of course, life isn't always ruled by tradition. If your parents are involved, get together with your fiancé and your family to determine a budget that is appropriate and comfortable. If the two of you are throwing the.wedding yourselves, work together to realistically figure out what you can afford; whether you can dip into savings or investments and still meet long-term goals such as buying property or starting a family. As fun as that reception can be, going into debt to pay for a wedding is not the best way to start a happy marriage.

Sadly, the fastest way to cut a budget is to eliminate guests. Not only does this cut into your gifts, but it can be awkward letting friends and family members know they are not invited to share in your joy. You can always explain that you are having a small wedding to prevent offending them, however, it may be better to compromise and sacrifice—if the money's not there you may not be able to get everything you want. However, if you set a budget right away, you'll be able to see in advance where you need to cut corners, and pinpoint ways to save money down the line, either by hosting the reception on a family property, creating your own invitations, assembling your own favor boxes or some other ingenious sleight of hand. The following list of potential expenses should help:

Reception
◎ Wedding planner fee
◎ Ceremony location fee
◎ Officiant's fee
◎ Marriage license
◎ Reception site fee
◎ Food/catering costs (tax, tip, etc.)
◎ Bar and beverages
◎ Wedding cake
◎ Rentals (tent, table, chairs. linens, etc.)
◎ Valet parking and transportation

Attire
◎ Bridal gown
◎ Headpiece/veil
◎ Lingerie
◎ Jewelry
◎ Bride's shoes and accessories
◎ Hair, makeup, manicure and pedicure
◎ Groom's ensemble
◎ Groom's shoes and accessories
◎ Wedding rings
◎ Alterations, dry cleaning and preservation

Flowers and Decor
◎ Ceremony flowers and decor
◎ Bouquets
◎ Flower girl basket and accessories
◎ Ring pillow
◎ Corsages and boutonnieres
◎ Reception centerpieces and decor

Gifts, Favors and Extras
◎ Maid of honor's gift
◎ Best man's gift
◎ Bridesmaids' gifts
◎ Groomsmen's gifts
◎ Child attendants' gifts
◎ Wedding couple's gifts
◎ Parents' gifts
◎ Welcome baskets for out-of-town guests
◎ Table favors
◎ Guest book and pen

Stationery
◎ Announcements/save-the-dates
◎ Invitations
◎ Calligraphy
◎ Postage
◎ Programs
◎ Seating charts/place cards
◎ Table numbers
◎ Menu cards
◎ Personalized stationery
◎ Thank-you notes

Photo/Video
◎ Photographer's fee
◎ Videographer's fee
◎ Wedding album package and photos
◎ Parents' album
◎ Additional prints

Music and Entertainment
◎ Ceremony music
◎ Cocktail hour soundtrack
◎ Reception music (band or DJ)

Other Expenses
◎ Honeymoon
◎ Luggage
◎ Video camera

>> The Bride & Groom

It goes without saying who're the two most important members of your wedding, and as the stars of the ceremony you'll want to be the best-dressed people in the room. More specifically, the bride should be the most beautiful woman anybody's ever seen, and, at the very least, the groom will want to be her dashing arm candy. It's easy to stress out about finding the perfect clothes, accessories, hair and makeup, but it's just as easy to have a great time choosing the perfect ensembles, whether you opt for the classic white gown and tux, or something less formal. The important thing is that you feel like a million bucks—you don't necessarily have to spend it. No amount of primping and preening will make you look better in those photographs than if you feel comfortable and confident.

In the days and weeks leading up to your wedding, don't let stress take over your relationship. Engage in some fun pre-wedding activities, such as food tastings and dance lessons. Just remember, you're not trying to be Fred and Ginger, you're just having a few laughs for a change when you step on each other's toes. When tension does start to mount, get a couples massage, or even take time to go to a spa and receive some head-to-toe pampering. When you're relaxed, and basking again in the glow of togetherness, seize the opportunity to pour this affection into your vows. Better now than when out-of-town family starts to arrive.

The Bride

When it comes to shopping around for that always-elusive perfect gown, searching through stacks of magazines can actually help you determine what you like. You'll see hundreds of beautiful dresses, but it will be easy to narrow down the selection if you have a realistic attitude and focus on those that will flatter your figure and be appropriate for the style of wedding you have chosen.

Once you've determined the styles of dress you prefer, make appointments at a couple of bridal salons and try on every one you can find. You aren't just trying the dresses; you are testing the salon itself. Are there nice people you're comfortable working with? Are they honest about what looks good on you? Do they have reliable tailoring services? Remember that ordering can take 4 to 6 months, before fittings, and bear in mind that bridal gowns tend to run smaller than off-the-rack clothing, so don't worry if you need to go up a size or two. A much bigger mistake is to buy a smaller size imagining you will fit into it by the time your wedding date rolls around (it's usually easy to take a dress in, but often impossible to let one out). If you are purchasing your gown online or ordering it from afar, it's extremely important to find a good tailor or seamstress who can do the fittings locally. As you are likely to lose weight as the big day gets closer, make sure your final fitting is within a week of the wedding day.

After you've purchased your gown, take some time to shop for appropriate lingerie. Depending on the dress, you may require a slip, petticoat, crinoline, bra, bustier, body shaper or a certain style panty. Then you can decide on hosiery, panty hose, stockings and garters (don't forget to add the extra garter for the traditional toss). Just remember to bring all the lingerie, shoes and accessories you will be wearing to your last couple of fittings, so you can see how it all feels and fits together.

Decide what sort of headpiece will look best with your gown, whether you will look better with a tiara, floral headband, hairpins or combs. Determine what style of jewelry will work, if any, and whether you would like to wear gloves. You may also wish to carry a handkerchief that hooks on to your bouquet (it will come in handy if you start to sniffle or cry). Have fun trying things out and imagining different combinations, and if you have the means, choose a couple of options so you have the freedom to decide at the last minute.

However, if you plan on wearing an intricate headpiece or tiara, try on and wear your headpiece for a few hours to make sure it won't give you a headache (besides, you get to feel like a princess for a little while). Likewise, wear your shoes inside for a few hours at a time to break them in and make sure they are comfortable enough to last through the ceremony and photo sessions. Which isn't to say the shoes you choose to walk down the aisle in necessarily have to be the same pair you wear during the much longer reception. With a floor-length gown, you may slip on a second pair of more comfortable shoes, ranging from white lace decorated sneakers to beaded ballet slippers. These will allow you to kick up your heels in wedded bliss and forgo the blisters.

As you assemble your outfit, be thinking about how you'd like to wear your hair, and in the meantime let it grow out a bit to keep your options open. If you are having any chemical hair treatments, like coloring, highlights or a perm, take care of this at least two weeks prior to the wedding, so your hair has time to recover and you have a safety window for damage control. If you're having your make-up professionally done, take a trial run at a shower or other event so your girlfirends can give you feedback. This way, you won't be disappointed with the results.

On the day of your wedding, wear a button-down shirt when you have your hair and makeup done so it can be easily removed when you are ready to get dressed. If, somehow, you wind up getting makeup or grease stains on your dress, gently rub a piece of chalk over the stain, wait a few minutes for the chalk to absorb then brush away the dust. A gum eraser works well to remove ink. These are the sort of products you'll want to include when you assemble your bridal emergency kit. Keep it close as your final hours as a single woman approach, and hope you don't need it.

Bridal Emergency Kit
◎ Safety pins
◎ Stain removers
◎ Small sewing kit
◎ Breath mints
◎ Extra makeup
◎ Aspirin or other pain relievers
◎ Tampons
◎ Clear nail polish to mend runs in stockings
◎ Reception shoes
◎ Hairpins, brush and spray
◎ Tissues

The Groom

In many cases, the groom may not know or care very much what his formalwear options are. However, if you rip out a few ideas for him from your bridal magazines, you can figure out what he favors. If he's agreeable to shopping a little bit, another way to check out different styles is to go to a tux rental shop. Even if you don't purchase there, you may get a good idea of the style that appeals to him (or you) most. If you're lucky (or unlucky) enough to have a groom who takes an active interest in his style selection, he'll want to decide whether he's more comfortable in a single-breasted, double-breasted, Mandarin, cutaway or a full-dress tailcoat, and whether he wants a notched, shawl or peaked collar.

Once the style is settled, it's easy to order the suit online and take it to a local tailor for alterations. Fitting should take place within three or four weeks of the wedding day, which will be a convenient time to purchase any coordinating accessories, such as shoes, socks, cufflinks, a cummerbund, tie, stud set or belt. As with the bride, he should wear his shoes inside for a few hours to make sure they fit. When you're sure they do, scuff the bottoms so he won't slip in them—putting those dance lessons to waste.

Grooms should also take note: buying the engagement ring isn't the end of your jewelry obligation. Picking out the wedding bands is something that should be done together. However, once they're ordered and properly sized, you might want to have them engraved. This will make them all the more special, and win you serious points on that honeymoon....

>> The Bridal Party

From the moment you announce your decision to wed, your friends and family will be waiting with bated breath for you to cast your supporting players. You should determine which people you would like to have stand with you and invite them to participate within a month of your engagement. Not only will this give them time to prepare for the tasks ahead, but they will prove invaluable in helping you through the weighty preliminary planning stages. Even if you've already known for years who your principal characters will be—people way too close to you to expect politeness or etiquette—finding creative ways to ask will be greatly appreciated. It can be as simple as a flower arrangement or a box of cigars, and as fun as a round of golf or margaritas and manicures; any gesture, big or small, can only heighten the heart-filled moment and cement the bond of friendship. If possible, bring your bridal party together as a group so everyone can get to feeling chummy well ahead of the requisite bachelor and bachelorette party planning.

Some roles, such as mother of the bride, are predetermined, but others will require a little soul searching and perhaps even a bit of tact. Asking the people you care about to play a role in your wedding is not merely an honor, but a responsibility. Your attendants will need to be up to the task, not only in the sense that they should be reliable, trustworthy and photogenic, but that they are willing and able to take on the sort of fiscal expense customarily attached to such prestigious positions, such as buying their own attire. In other words, you can't necessarily count on your wild and disorganized best friends to get it together for this. However, there are many different ways to give your loved ones a sense of involvement with your nuptials, so peruse the following roles to help figure out how to spread the wealth, and share the burdens.

Matron or Maid of Honor

Whether it's your closest friend, sister, mother or daughter, the maid of honor will be your chief lady-in-waiting from the initial planning through to the last-minute preparations. You'll want to choose wisely, but also from your heart, because the chances are this woman will be forced to suffer all of your stresses, tempers and insecurities right alongside you. Customary maid of honor duties include:

◎ Assisting in the wedding planning
◎ Helping to choose bridesmaid attire
◎ Organizing bridal shower and bachelorette party
◎ Keeping all bridesmaids organized and informed
◎ Helping the bride get ready on the wedding day
◎ Holding the groom's wedding ring during the ceremony
◎ Holding the bridal bouquet during the ceremony
◎ Arranging the veil and train during the ceremony
◎ Signing the marriage license or Ketubah
◎ Giving a toast at the rehearsal dinner or reception
◎ Helping the bride leave the reception
◎ Keeping a record of gifts at showers and events

Best Man

This most prestigious male honor should be bestowed upon the groom's closest and most reliable friend, or even his brother, son or father. It should be someone who cares a great deal about both of you, and will selflessly take on any arduous task to help you stay organized and on schedule. Typical best man duties include:

- Assisting in wedding and related event planning
- Helping select formalwear for groomsmen
- Picking up and returning tuxedo rentals
- Making sure all of the groomsmen get their attire on time
- Handing out the boutonnieres
- Throwing the bachelor party
- Holding the bride's wedding ring during the ceremony
- Signing the marriage license or ketubah
- Handing out payments to vendors on the wedding day
- Helping coordinate transportation
- Walking the maid of honor down the aisle
- Making the first toast at the reception
- Helping groom get ready to leave the reception

Groomsmen & Bridesmaids

There are no set standards for how many groomsmen and bridesmaids stand with you, if any at all. And, though people traditionally like to balance both genders, there's no harm in an asymmetrical bridal party. These attendants are usually friends, brothers, sisters, and other close relatives, and provide the opportunity to include close women on the groom's side, as well as favorite men of the bride. Though it can be nice to reciprocate, you shouldn't necessarily feel pressured to ask someone simply because you participated in their wedding. These attendants will perform various duties, usually in support of the best man and maid of honor, but should be available for any additional tasks that might arise, such as organizing parking or running small errands at the last minute.

Ushers

Assigning ushers is a nice way to include someone who is not in the ceremony itself, especially teen family members or friends of the groom. You'll typically want to provide one usher for every 50 guests, and their primary jobs will be to instruct people when and where they should be seated, and to escort family members to their reserved seats.

You can also ask ushers to hand out programs, direct guests to sign the guest book and distribute the wedding toss, bubbles or sparklers.

Junior Bridesmaids

Young women who are too old to be a flower girl, yet not old enough to handle the responsibilities of a bridesmaid may be asked to serve as a junior bridesmaid. Usually little sisters or teen relatives play this sweet, mostly honorary role, and their dresses should be similar in color and/or style to those of the bridesmaids. They, too, may be called upon to hand out programs or direct people to the guest book.

Flower Girl

A little girl close to the two of you will fill this most precious role, whether she's your daughter or that of a close friend or relative. Since young girls love to be a part of pretty ceremonies, there's no need to play favorites—having more than one will just be that much more adorable. The flower girl's parents will be responsible for her attire, but the bride should give direction as to what kind or color dress to purchase, and provide the basket and any flowers or petals.

Ring Bearer

For the little brother, cousin, nephew or son, this is a sweet and prideful role that really only requires the child be old enough to walk and take direction. Traditionally, he carries the bride's and groom's rings down the aisle on a pillow, but today, often symbolic rings are carried by the cute little tyke, just in case. He generally wears attire similar to that of the groomsmen.

Mother of the Bride

The mother of the bride has always been there to support her daughter. Helping the bride choose her attire for all wedding related events probably won't be the least of her contributions. This will hopefully be a joyous time to share with your mother, and should allow her the opportunity to bond with her future son-in-law. In the meantime shopping together for her dress can provide some great mother-daughter bonding time. Try and make it a fun event.

Father of the Bride

Traditionally, the father of the bride is responsible for paying for the wedding and walking the bride down the aisle and giving her away— arguably the toughest wedding job of all! You may want to pick out his outfit, or enlist your mother to do so, and probably provide a handkerchief to prepare for the great likelihood that one or both of you will get misty-eyed during the procession. If your father has passed on, or is otherwise unavailable to give you away, asking a beloved male relative, role model or friend of the family to fill this role will surely lead to one of the highlights of his life.

Parents of the Groom

The parents of the groom can be as involved as they are invited to be by the engaged couple. Often the parents walk their son down the aisle and participate in the processional. Their commitment usually entails throwing the rehearsal dinner and assuming some of the groom's costs, although offering to help out with the bride's jewelry or headpiece can be a gracious gesture and a lovely start to the new filial relationship.

Officiant

Selecting someone to preside over your vows will be an easy task if you are getting married in your hometown and have a religious leader who has known you or your family for quite some time. But if this isn't the case, you will need to interview and select someone who will bring the right amount of religious and/or emotional meaning for the bride, groom and families, preferably someone with dignity, charisma and the respect of the couple as well as the community. It can be tricky these days to find the right person, given that the bride and groom and your respective families may have quite different religious backgrounds and beliefs, so make sure to make this a thoughtful joint decision, gauging how important the decision is to all interested parties. Some couples even choose to have two officiants preside, making sure both religions are represented. Mostly, you'll want your officiant to be somebody you both feel comfortable with.

Usually, religious leaders and community officials accept an officiant's fee for their time counseling the betrothed couple, preparing and performing a unique ceremony. If you are having trouble compromising upon a specific denomination, or have opted for a secular wedding, a popular contemporary choice is to enlist a mutual friend of the bride and groom to perform a somewhat less ritualistic ceremony. This can be the person who introduced you, someone of similar significance, or even just someone who has a pleasant speaking voice and a humorous demeanor. Web sites like www.ulc.org and www.spiritualhumanism.org offer to ordain someone online in an instant, and depending on where you reside, the state may authorize any civilian to preside over an official ceremony, presuming the proper paperwork is filled out.

Other Special Roles

If you have additional special friends and relations you wish to include, here are a few time-tested ways to involve them in your ceremony or reception without requiring any sort of arduous commitment.

◎ Request a toast at the rehearsal dinner
◎ Ask them to light a candle at the ceremony (perhaps in memory of a late friend or relative)
◎ Enlist them to read a passage or poem during the ceremony
◎ Have them hold the chuppah (in a Jewish ceremony)
◎ Invite them to say a blessing at the reception
◎ Entreat them to host a post-wedding brunch
◎ Let them have a special dance with the bride or groom at the reception

Outfitting Your Attendants

Ultimately, the bride has final say over who wears what to her wedding—well, when it comes to her attendants, if not her guests. Of course, in most cases, it's up to the members of the bridal party to pay for their own attire, so it's deemed considerate to give them at least some say in the matter.

It's easy enough to dress the best man and groomsmen if you're outfitting them formally, as there's always the option to rent rather than buy matching tuxedos. Have the best man keep strict tabs on the rental shop, though, as you don't want to wind up with mismatching bow ties or cummerbunds. In any case, it's customary to consider what the groom is wearing and have his attendants follow suit. This may be more difficult in casual or semi-formal settings, where you may have to settle for matching ties or, say, Hawaiian shirts. Just keep reminding yourself that it's way more important to you than it is to them, and feel free to insist upon the garments you have chosen.

Your female attendants could prove a little more delicate. You'll definitely have to consult your maid of honor, who may demand (and possibly deserve) a more distinctive dress than your coordinated bridesmaids. That is, presuming you do decide to put your bridesmaids in matching dresses, which is, again, entirely up to you. It's a safe bet that when your girls accept the offer to stand with you, they'll reserve a slight bit of dread that they'll wind up in pastel ruffles that obscure or distort their figures, though in truth, most modern brides don't really want that. If you're feeling particularly generous, you may wish to work with them to select dresses they actually like enough even to wear again. In fact, many shops will offer several styles of dress in the same color and fabric, allowing each of your bridesmaids to choose a design that flatters her particular body type without deviating from your dedicated scheme. Obviously, though, you don't want any of your ladies in waiting to outshine the radiant beauty and elegance of the bride, so be careful not to pick anything too appealing!

Thanking Your Attendants With Gifts

As they've celebrated and suffered with you, have gone the distance and spared no expense to ensure your wedding and the months leading up to it are memorable and fun, it's only right that you reciprocate with a gracious gesture of your own. To begin with, when you are in the midst of the stressful planning stages, make sure to be thoughtful and acknowledge those helping you along the way—after all, at some point, every bride can be a lot to tolerate. When it's all over, though, be sure to thank your upstanding men and women with something a little more concrete.

Customarily, attendant gifts are given anywhere from a week before the wedding to the day of, often at the rehearsal dinner. Although there are certain gifting standards, any thoughtfulness will be truly appreciated by those you love, whether you give a traditional gift spruced up with a touch of personalization, or a handmade, handpicked or extravagant thank-you. That said, these guys and girls have purchased special attire, thrown you a party, gotten you a gift and probably spent money you don't even know about—in other words, don't be cheap. Recognize them with something special that they will truly use and enjoy. Here are some ideas:

For the Girls

◎ Jewelry they can wear at the wedding
◎ A beautiful evening bag
◎ Silver engraved picture frame (then supply them with a photo from the wedding later)
◎ Spa gift certificate
◎ Romantic dinner for two at a nice local restaurant
◎ iPod with all of your favorite songs loaded on it
◎ Engraved silver compact
◎ Monogrammed tote bag to carry all necessities to the wedding
◎ Digital camera

For the Guys

◎ A round of golf and personalized golf balls
◎ Engraved cufflinks to wear on the big day
◎ Watch
◎ Cocktail set
◎ Concert or sporting event tickets
◎ Massage gift certificate
◎ iPod loaded with music
◎ Digital camera
◎ Monogrammed pocketknife, pen or money clip
◎ Poker set
◎ Flask

Ring Bearer & Flower Girl

◎ Backpack filled with toys and games
◎ Disposable camera
◎ Picture frame or album
◎ Stuffed animal

Parents

◎ Sterling picture frame with a wedding photo to be given later
◎ A night of dinner and dancing
◎ Theater tickets

>> Spreading the Word

Once you've agreed to tie the knot, you'll probably want to run out and tell the world. Of course, as with all things wedding, there's a suggested way to going about announcing your joy. Although word of mouth will probably get the job done, that would interfere with the opportunity to send people cute stationery. Of course, it all can get very complicated when you realize you need to formulate a guest list, get everybody's address, stamp and label envelopes and collect RSVPs.

The first thing we'd suggest is to keep very detailed records of everybody on your guest list. For each person, collect and record an address, phone number and email address, as well as whether you've sent him or her a save-the-date, invite and thank you card, and whether you've received an RSVP or gift. As long as you maintain this sort of address book, you should be able to more or less manage the following without hassle.

Engagement Announcements

If you choose to send announcements, this will pretty much be the first thing you do once you get engaged, and it will make your decision all seem a little more official-like. Who you include in this first round of correspondence is pretty much a combination of who you want to tell and who you know how to reach. Give word by phone or in person to your family first, then your friends, and they will probably chip in a few addresses of old family friends you might not have considered.

Though you'll probably want to keep your announcements simple and to the point (you haven't even begun to set a date yet), there's no saying you can't have a little fun with it. Announcements generally consist of postcards letting people know you got engaged to this specific person on such-and-such date, but there's always the option to have the card personalized with your photographs, or to make them yourself with a simple word processor program and a printer. You'll have plenty of time to fashion some more stylish invitations later....

The Guest List

The next step you want to take is to assemble a guest list. This is possibly the most difficult and arduous task of the entire planning process. You should have four lists to work from: the bride's list, the groom's list and a list from each set of parents. This will give you an initial idea of just how many people might want to celebrate with the two of you. From there you may add—but will more likely eliminate—names. The elimination process is difficult, as you'll hate to leave some people out. However, the cost of receptions usually multiply fast based on a price-per-person basis, and when you compare your guest list to your working budget, you'll be motivated to trim the excess. Try to limit the number of plus-ones on your guest list and entice single friends with the idea they might make a connection on the dance floor. Next, consider sending wedding announcements, rather than invitations, to certain out-of-touch friends or distant relations. Also, you may contemplate having a separate, informal reception and limit the actual wedding to close friends and family.

Once you've broken it down as far as you're willing to go, split your master list into two final lists. The first will be the must invite list. Since there is no way to leave these people off your guest list, send them all invitations roughly eight weeks prior to your wedding, and request RSVPs within two weeks. Once you begin to get RSVPs back, any negative replies will simply open up more spots for the people on list #2. Send invites to those on the second list about six weeks prior to the event, and hope that your math was correct and that, when it all adds up, you haven't exceeded your limit.

Save-the-Date Cards

Once you've set the date, the first word those lucky souls who have made your guest list may receive comes in the form of a save-the-date card. Again, these are typically simple postcards, or themed notes you may print yourself, and not likely coordinated with your actual invitations. Save the dates are often sent out about six months before the wedding, usually if it is taking place during a busy time of the year (holidays, summer vacation, etc.), or to give your guests time to make travel arrangements for a destination wedding. These offer your date and a location, and is also an opportunity to let out-of-town guests know about your wedding web page, where they can find information about group travel and hotel rates.

Publishing a Web Page

Clearly, this is not a part of the process that's deeply mired in tradition. Nevertheless, the number of web page styles and hosting options have grown quickly over the past decade, and putting your wedding information online will be easy even for the computer inept, usually just requiring you to sign up with a wedding web site (as evidenced by our helpful sites section on page 46).

This proves an excellent way to present detailed maps of how to reach your ceremony and reception sites (saving you the cost of printing invitation inserts), link directly to your online bridal registries, link out-of-town guests to group airfare and lodging options and generally share useful or fun information about the betrothed couple and local activities surrounding the wedding.

The Invitations

At last it's time to select your invitations, and the options are no less than infinite, particularly if you peruse our Wedding Shops section and browse the more than fifty online stationers listed there. Invites are the first thing that will actually get people excited about your wedding. They remind your guests the big date approaches and prompt them to secure their place at the table. Traditionally, both the bride and groom's parents are presented as the hosts, inviting guests to join the "blessed matrimony" or "sacred union" of the named couple, and offering details about the ceremony's time and location, as well as the reception. Enclosures may include maps, RSVP cards, stamped RSVP envelopes and notice of any preferred bridal registries and/or wedding web pages.

Of course, this is merely a common guideline. Even following the traditional path, invitations provide a lot of room for creativity and personal flourishes. After all, they don't just provide information, but set the tone for the type of wedding your guests will be attending. Hence, if you plan a lavish, formal affair, you'll want your invitations to be classic and elegant, with hand calligraphy and quality papers and vellum sheets to separate the enclosures. Casual weddings will warrant more whimsical stationery, presenting the information with a sense of humor. Every conceivable style is available to anyone who looks hard enough, and if you play your cards right, your guests will actually be able to figure out what to wear based on the presentation of the invites alone (though, if there's any ambiguity, you might just inform them directly).

When ordering invitations, a good rule of thumb is to purchase at least 20 more than you think you'll need, and while you're at it try to order matching thank-you notes, and monogrammed stationery. This will also be a good time to look out for any other items you may want in the future, such as wedding announcements, menus, programs, match books, napkins, coasters, guest towels, place cards and table numbers, which will be ordered closer to the wedding day. Likewise, this is the time to book a professional calligrapher, if you want one, especially if you have a large order. An alternative would be to buy calligraphy font software to print out cards yourself. Heck, even if you don't intent to use any calligraphy whatsoever, creating your own invitations is a great way to save money and get exactly the look you desire.

>> Taking Care of Business

By now, you've probably gotten the point that organizing a wedding is a huge undertaking, requiring the efforts of more than two people, or even five or six. That's why an entire industry has sprung up around event planning and why you will, in all likelihood, contract at least a couple of different vendors to help make your wedding a success. We've put together a list of common vendors and how to make the most of the services they provide. Remember, although they are in the business of satisfying customers, it is merely a professional endeavor for them, so getting the results you desire may require that you effectively and decisively communicate your wants and needs and include them, in no uncertain terms, in your contracts. This is definitely not the romantic part of wedding planning.

Wedding Planner

If you are going to be working with a wedding planner, this is the first person you'll want to hire for a couple of reasons. First, he or she will help you coordinate a schedule and keep all of your options and decisions in order. Second, a good planner will prove an excellent access point to all the other vendors you need, and though hiring one may add to your budget now, he or she will have resources and discounts that may save you money and stress later. Begin looking for one as soon as possible, and interview at least two or three to find one that you feel you can comfortably communicate with. In any case, get references and look at photos of the consultant's recent events.

Florist

When it comes to flowers, it always helps to have an expert on hand, particularly someone with direct access to local nurseries. When meeting with a florist, discuss colors, bouquets, decor for the ceremony, reception centerpieces, bridal party flowers, petals for the wedding night suite and any other idea you might have. Break out your magazines and show them looks you like, and discuss lighting and linens if necessary. Be sure to mention any allergies suffered by members of your bridal party (handkerchiefs should be reserved for tears of joy).

Once you've covered the basics, go over your floral budget and be realistic—you can add the beauty of flowers at any price! When your terms are settled, make sure the contract spells out the specific flowers you have selected, both color and number. Follow this up with a meeting one month before your wedding in order to see how everything will look together with the flowers in season. If any changes need to be made, you can make them then.

Caterer

Selecting a caterer can be a fun and tasty activity for the bride and groom to do together. Seek out a variety of caterers and sample their food extensively (don't forget the dessert!). When you meet with them, be sure to address all of the specifics. Are they licensed and certified? Will they provide liquor and are they licensed to serve it? Do they have liability insurance? What is their cancellation policy? How much do they charge for overtime?

When you discuss the menu, parse out every detail, such as what sort of appetizers they'll serve during your cocktail hour, what sort of children's menu they'll provide, how they might address special dietary needs, what beverages will be served with dinner, which style of serving-ware will be used and what sort of timing is required for food preparation. You may be able to save money on a waiting staff by opting for a buffet, but either way you should determine at which point they'll require the final head count so the right amount of food is served. Once you've finalized the menu, don't be afraid to schedule a second tasting. In fact, you might want to factor this in to your pre-wedding diet.

Photographer & Videographer

When you think back on it ten years, one year, a week or even a day later, your entire wedding day will seem like a blur. This is why it's wise to hire a good photographer to document the occasion. Both the staged pictures of the bridal party and the action shots of the ceremony will serve to remind you what a fantastic and beautiful time it was, from your guests' arrival to the good-byes at the end of the night. Make sure the photographer takes both color and black-and-white photos. If you can afford it, hire a second photographer (often his or her assistant). One will take the more formal and posed shots, while the other is there to capture the candid moments. Another, more fun and popular way to collect this second group of photographs is to provide your guests with disposable wedding cameras. They will use these to take shots that allow you to see the good times through their eyes, which can be priceless.

You may also wish to hire a videographer to capture all the special moments, from the procession to the getaway car driving away from the reception. A good one will stay inconspicuous while recording the action, and will include full editing services as well as the master tapes in the total package. You may also ask the videographer to record interviews with your guests, which you should discuss in detail beforehand.

Before hiring either professional, look at samples of work, discuss styles you like and when the photos will be taken. Make sure you feel comfortable with the photographer you choose–the more comfortable you are, the better the photos will be. If there are particular poses or specific shots you want, make a list and include then in the contract. Get everything in writing, along with a guarantee that the professional you hire doesn't send a protégé in his or her place, which is not uncommon in the industry.

Bakery

Selecting your wedding cake is another opportunity for you and your fiancé to go on taste testing dates and to cheat on your diets. Start your research by perusing your bridal magazines, then visit several bakeries and look at their books to get an idea of what you want for your wedding cake. Cake decorating technology has improved to the point that you should actually be able to incorporate your personal style into the baked good, which in itself may be a good reason to get creative and not be stuck to traditional styles.

Once you have found a couple of cake designs you like, schedule some tastings and find out whether your visual masterpiece actually pleases the palate. When you have found the right one, it's a simple matter to set up a contract, being sure to double-check all of the important details with the bakery. Aside from the where and the when, they will need to know how many people the cake will serve, and whether you will be garnishing the cake with fresh flowers, in which case you might want them to coordinate with your florist.

If, for some reason, you and the groom cannot agree on a certain flavor of cake, you can order a second one to serve as the groom's cake. Usually the groom's cake is richer, such as chocolate or red velvet, and it often deviates in form as well. You can let the groom choose this cake himself, or save it as a surprise for him. Either way, your guests win, because they get to have both.

Musicians

You may want to hire live musicians for the ceremony, the reception or both. For ceremonies, solo performers or small, acoustic ensembles are usually preferred, traditionally involving organs, harps or other classical string instruments. For the reception, you'll usually want something a bit more upbeat; after all, they have to get and keep the party going. With either option you'll want to ask for references, to see a video of their work, or even to see if you can peek into an upcoming event where they will be performing. Obviously, song selection is a big consideration, and any group will need to be willing and able to play your special requests.

A DJ may prove to be a better value, especially one who brings along any needed equipment, with the added benefit that he or she can easily include popular songs and personal favorites to keep the crowd dancing. If you will be hiring a DJ, make sure to ask for a playlist of available music to choose from, and be explicit about vetoing songs you don't like or approve of. Some DJs will also provide lighting, which may be worth considering, depending on your space. Given the proliferation of mixing equipment in the past decade, you might even be lucky enough to have a friend who is willing to perform.

Regardless of what sort of entertainment you hire, be sure to find out ahead of time how long they will perform, how much they charge for overtime (and at when it kicks in), how many breaks they will require, how many meals they will need, what sort of recorded music will play when they take breaks and what they will wear. You may also wish the DJ or band leader to serve as MC to your wedding events—if so, determine this ahead of time and issue instructions accordingly. This contract needs to be very specific. You will also need to coordinate with the reception site to find out its cut-off time and what restrictions there may be on volume. It would be a shame for the police to show up uninvited.

Venues & Equipment Rentals
Hiring a venue can be quite easy, or quite hard, depending on how commonly the space is used for such events, and just how popular it turns out to be. There are many user-friendly venues in any city that routinely cater to wedding ceremonies and receptions. In fact, they'll often provide food and drinks, seating and table service, which can make a lot of planning incredibly easy. One potential drawback of such a site is that it may book a second event on the same day as yours, either before or after yours. You'll want to be very specific about exactly when and for how long this space is open to you and your planning committee.

Holding the ceremony and reception in a single location makes transportation and parking easier all the way around, but this will rarely provide a satisfactory location for both parts of your event. When selecting different venues, keep interim travel in mind, especially if guests will be force to endure heavy traffic, construction or bad roads. A destination wedding, in particular, should probably be pretty self-contained, particularly if it's held in a foreign country.

In the event the venue cannot provide seating, tables, outdoor shade, linens, etc., you will need to contract outside companies to provide such equipment. Especially if you're not planning a weekday wedding, try to book these well in advance because, coincidentally, they seem to book up fast on weekends.

Lodging & Accommodations
If you are having your wedding at a hotel, oftentimes a bridal suite comes as part of the package. Otherwise, if you don't want to go home after the wedding, you'll may still want to book a nice room at a hotel close by where you two can escape and collapse for your first night as a happily married couple. Book this far enough in advance that you can get your choice of room, and don't hesitate to mention the reason you'll be celebrating.

While you're at it, you may want to see if the hotel, or other ones close by, will offer group rates on rooms for your out-of-town guests, or at least reserve a block of rooms for patrons of your event. You'll definitely want to do this early on so you may include lodging information with save-the-date cards, on your wedding website or in your invitations. If you're feeling thoughtful, you may create welcome baskets for the out-of-town guests and have them delivered to their rooms. These baskets can include snacks, drinks, a list of local attractions, a local specialty or souvenir, a local map, a schedule of wedding-related events and the contact phone number of someone in the wedding party. If there are a great number of out-of-town guests, you may also want to arrange shuttle transportation to the wedding and related events. You also may wish to make baby-sitting services available, particularly if you want parents of young children to celebrate freely with you.

Transportation

It's not usually viewed as a high-priority expense, but there may in fact be several transportation options you wish to explore for your wedding. The first, selfishly, will be a limousine, car service or rental car to whisk you to and away from the reception in style. Selecting such a service will be based on price and preference, and it's usually something that will keep the groom and best man busy and out of your hair.

The other services you may provide very much have your guests in mind. If your reception site is in a difficult place to park, for example, you might do well to hire a parking valet service, and may discover there's one used to working that area. Otherwise, you may contract a bus to shuttle guests from a hotel or outside parking source. This offers the added benefit that you can serve alcohol and not have to worry about your guests driving afterwards.

Personal Business

There are a variety of small personal, legal and financial details both the bride and groom must contend with when joining their lives together. Different regions and financial institutions will have different policies regarding your specific situation, but here is a general list of tasks to consider. Remember to keep excellent documentation, including certified copies of all official documents. In fact, order several certified copies of your marriage license, as they will most certainly be required for other tasks further down the list.

For Bride & Groom
◎ Register for a marriage license
◎ Change insurance policies
◎ Set up joint bank accounts
◎ Get blood tests
◎ Change of address
◎ Arrange and sign prenuptial agreement
◎ Send wedding announcements to local newspapers

For the Bride
◎ Name change application
◎ Change name on passport
◎ Change name on social security card
◎ Change name on driver's license

>> Related Events

The party doesn't necessarily start with the walk down the aisle, nor does it finish with the bride and groom driving away in a car dangling tin cans. There are many surrounding events your friends and family may be excited about, and although you don't traditionally have to plan most of them yourselves, being aware of each one at least gives you a chance to keep tabs on the progress of your loved ones.

Engagement Party

Once you've announced the big news, a family member or close friend may wish to throw you an engagement party—in fact, a few of them may step forward to do so. It's pretty much your job to put them in touch with each other, contribute to the guest list and make sure the groom shows up. This party should take place within two months of the engagement and not less than six months before the wedding, its purpose to start the celebration and give friends and family a chance to meet and start getting used to the idea of being in each others' lives for the long haul.

Bridal Shower

The bridal shower will be the first chance for the girls to get together to heap presents and advice upon the bride-to-be. Usually taking place between one and four months before the wedding, who plans and attends may vary depending on your own wishes and your family's traditions, but it's usually less intimate and less wild than the subsequent bachelorette party. Actually, some brides choose to have two separate showers; one thrown by family and family friends, another planned by her close friends and contemporaries. In both cases, having a guest list prepared for your hostesses will make their jobs a lot easier.

Although traditionally just for the girls, in recent years co-ed showers have become a common trend, largely depending on the sort of gift registry involved. For example, customary registries of domestic and household products, once considered a woman's domain, are now recognized as bilateral, and the groom-to-be may wish to be present to receive gifts. On the other hand, another trend of theme showers may elicit different sorts of registries, such as for lingerie, in which case restricting invitations to women once again seems prudent.

Bachelor & Bachelorette Parties

Of course, there's quite a longstanding tradition of pre-wedding parties that separate the sexes. Bachelor and bachelorette parties are arranged by the best man and maid of honor, respectively, and though the groom and bride are quite clearly the guests of honor for these lighthearted and even cheeky events, a case could be made that these parties' existence are actually more toward the benefit of the guests who attend. Both are intended to celebrate the individual's last remaining days of single life, and consequently may prove threatening to either or both prospective spouses, although usually the "threats" are without merit.

Bachelor parties, in particular, retain the stigma of featuring stag films, strippers and other, unmentionable misadventures. However, the truth is, most modern bachelor parties are relatively low key by mythical standards, often involving recreational activities enjoyed by the groom and his friends, including golf, fishing, camping, road trips and poker. Granted, these activities may merely serve as a precursor to other pursuits, beginning with alcohol and never again discussed by those in attendance, but any indiscretions are usually perpetuated by the groom's cronies, part of a bizarre ritual meant to provoke feelings of loyalty and discomfort.

If anything, bachelorette parties are only gaining ground on their counterparts in terms of reputation, and if the array of products available at contemporary bachelorette niche retailers are any indication, women may actively be attempting to surpass men on the raunchy scale. Generally, though, this party is an excuse for the girls to get together, en masse, to play games, hold scavenger hunts, roast the bride-to-be and occasionally attract the attention of bystanders.

Rehearsal Dinner

The rehearsal dinner is traditionally hosted by the groom's family, and is usually held the night before the wedding, immediately following the rehearsal of the ceremony. The guests should include immediate family, the bridal party, out-of-town guests and anyone special you want to recognize or include. This can be casual or formal, from a barbecue, luau, and karaoke to a posh, catered meal in cocktail attire—regardless, it should be fun. This proves an excellent opportunity for people from different parts of your lives to get to know one another, roast the couple and give toasts (the more here, the fewer at the reception). This may also be a good time for the bride and groom to present their attendants with gifts of appreciation.

After Party

Chances are, whatever venue you choose, there will come a point in the evening where your lease on the place expires, your wait staff and musicians clock out and the coffee runs out. The party will be over. However, you should be able to count on certain of your guests to keep the party going even after the lights turn out. Arrange to see if any friends wish to host an after party, or encourage late-night guests as a group to go bowling, have a beach bonfire, play poker or go out to a club for karaoke or more dancing. Most likely, by this time the bride and groom are past the point of exhaustion, but even if you only put in an appearance it might be fun to witness the hilarious aftermath of your open bar.

Post-Wedding Brunch

On the morning following the wedding, it will occur to everyone that all the out-of-town family and friends are still gathered in one convenient location. Since breakfast may be too early for some late-night revelers, guests customarily get together for a group brunch on the morning following the reception. This may be hosted at the home of local friends or family members, or a favorite restaurant that is able and willing to cater to what may quickly turn into a large party. The beauty of this shared meal is that it usually lacks the frenetic pace of a wedding reception, giving relations and acquaintances a chance to reminisce about old times, as well as about the night before.

>> The Honeymoon

In case you were wondering what the immediate reward is for all the hard work you've put in to plan this wedding, look no further than the honeymoon. Not only is this the respite you have earned from your effort and expense, but it will be an opportunity for the two of you to get to know each other as husband and wife, away from all the social responsibilities and daily obligations of your regular life.

Half the fun—well, okay, maybe a quarter of the fun—is tossing around ideas about where you might like to go. It's a big world, and there are many things to think about when considering a destination: how tired will you be after the wedding? Do you want an activity-packed adventure, or an indulgent rest by the beach? Do you want to go someplace where the weather's warmer than it is at home, or would you prefer a cool locale where you can stay indoors to keep each other warm? Ultimately, your budget might play a big factor in determining how far you go and for how long. Fortunately, in the last few years honeymoon registries have grown in popularity and acceptance, so if you already have enough dinnerware and bed linens, you might consider subsidizing your dream vacation with the help of your loved ones.

Regardless of how you plan to pay for it, if you are planning a far away escape or a multiple destination journey, it is best to plan early and book well in advance. Not only will this ensure you can find lodging in popular destinations, but you will almost always secure a better price. Whether you book online or through a travel agent, record your confirmation numbers, keep paper documentation of your itinerary and make sure someone at home has a copy, in case of emergency. Find out soon whether you need any special visas or immunizations, so you can get everything in order before the last minute. Brides should take into account that if you haven't had time to legally change your name, you should make your arrangements under your maiden name, to be on the safe side.

For an extensive assortment of online travel tips, booking options, vacation packages and retailers, watch out for **thepurplebook**: The Definitive Guide to Exceptional Online Shopping, 2007 edition, or simply visit:

www.thepurplebook.com

>> Keepsakes & Preservation

Even as each new moment passes, your memories of the happiest day of your life may start to fade, a function of the adrenaline, the sheer number of well-wishers clamoring for your attention and, probably, the booze. Fortunately, you can insert a few lovely mnemonic devices throughout the day that will serve as reminders of how you were feeling at one moment, or who you were talking to the next, not the least of which will be the photographs and video taken.

Traditional Keepsakes

Any durable item may serve as a memento if you attach enough meaning to it. However, there are a few time-tested keepsakes that help capture the moment of specific wedding activities, beginning with something old, something new, something borrowed and something blue. These are the sort of things you'll want to store in a box in you closet, to be opened on anniversaries, to show your children or just whenever you get to feeling nostalgic.

The ceremony itself will mostly be filled with words, sights, sounds and smells, and it might seem the thing you most remember will be the beating of your own heart. Saving the program will help you retain a sense of order from the dreamlike jumble of noise and sound. Your headpiece, tussie-mussie (bouquet holder) and veil may provoke more personal memories of getting ready with your attendants, your walk up the aisle and those first moments standing before your groom. Keeping the handkerchief you carried might even conjure up the emotions you felt as your eyes welled up with tears, or the giggles got the best of you.

Wedding cake charms, cake servers and cake toppers will remind you of—you guessed it—the wedding cake. Cutting the cake usually signifies some of the first moments you can finally loosen up a little bit and start to celebrate with your loved ones. The sense of relief will probably be strong enough to feel it all over again, years later.

Garters and bouquets present a quandary, because although they can make for tremendous keepsakes, you will have tossed them away to the single men and women in attendance. If you are determined to save these reminders of joyful times, always remember you can buy two garters (you do have two legs), keeping one of them for your keepsake box. The bouquet might not be so simple—chances are the woman who catches it will have worked hard for her spoils, and may not be willing to give it up so readily. Of course, she will most likely be a close friend, and fully understanding if you ask the right way. She can always plan to keep her own bouquet sometime down the line; after all, luck is on her side.

Keeping a guest book, or guest registry, may not immediately seem like the most necessary component of your wedding day, but reading the personal greetings and endearments later will almost certainly bring a fond tear to your eye, however silly, sappy and sentimental they might be. Of course, you can keep this right beside your wedding album, which you'll most likely make after the honeymoon, when you can clean up after the long months of planning, assembling the various paper artifacts from your journey, and favorite pictures from the day that ultimately did turn out to be the dream you always expected.

Preservation

Some keepsakes aren't quite so ready to last in a box in your closet. With these more delicate mementos, you will need to take special steps to prepare through the years of your marriage. You should be able to find many resources online and off (see Tips & Tools starting on page 45), but here are preliminary steps to take.

Preserving Your Cake

Saving the top layer of your wedding cake to eat on your first anniversary is traditionally good luck. However, if not done right it can turn into an experience of extremely bad taste! The following steps will help, although you'll probably want to assign a family member of one of your bridesmaids this responsibility.

◎ Wrap the cake tightly in plastic wrap
◎ Wrap it again in aluminum foil
◎ Place the wrapped cake in an airtight container
◎ Place the airtight container in the back of your freezer
◎ Thaw in fridge 48 hours, then 2-3 hours at room temperature

Preserving Your Gown

There are products specially designed to safely store your gown for future brides or even the next generation, and everything coming into contact with the gown should be acid free. Many reputable dry cleaning establishments offer a preservation service, as do some bridal salons. After your wedding day, have your gown professionally cleaned. Once correctly packaged, store it in a cool dry place. If you take the correct steps, you'll keep an heirloom that will retain its original beauty for years to come.

>> Tips & Tools

A healthy combination of forethought, common sense, organization and the internet may be all the tools you need to throw the best wedding for your buck. Take advantage of the following resources, pointers and checklists as you use the rest of the book to find the products you want and need.

General Tips

As your wedding approaches, you need to prepare yourself for the likelihood that something will go wrong, if only because high heels, a floor-length gown, a veil and the fact that you will probably drink champagne on an empty stomach are a dangerous combination. However, you can avoid some pitfalls and catastrophes with a little forethought. Here are few pointers that should keep trouble at bay, and prevent regret.

◎ Get everything in writing! Once you have negotiated and agreed upon terms, make sure all of your vendors have every specific detail spelled out in their contracts.

◎ Create a wedding notebook, and take it with you to all of your appointments. Keep a calendar, business cards, price quotes and photos of things you like. Take notes at all meetings.

◎ Shop around and do your homework. Check the references of all vendors, or go to events to see their work in progress. Don't grab the first thing that comes along; there's always better quality or more affordable options available. Ask vendors for discounts. It doesn't hurt to ask—the worst they can say is no.

◎ Place a cap on certain expenses. When you create your budget, know there are some areas you may need to go over on, so place a firm cap on those items that are less important.

◎ Open a separate bank account to cover wedding costs and dedicate one credit card for wedding expenses. This will help you keep track of what you are spending. You might want to sign up for a new card that provides you with frequent flier miles or other benefits to put toward your honeymoon.

◎ Pay with a credit card whenever possible—if something should go wrong, you will have more financial protection.

◎ Write thank-you notes as your gifts arrive; before the wedding.

◎ Bring food and beverages to the room where you spend the morning getting ready, or you will go all day on an empty stomach, leaving you tired, irritable and possibly feeling sick for the happiest moment of your life.

Helpful Sites

The web offers more than shopping to help your wedding come together beautifully. We found the following online resources to help with a variety of research and tasks.

General Wedding Resources

eWedding.com

OrganicWeddings.com

TheKnot.com

TheWeddingExperience.com

WeddingChannel.com

WeddingPearl.com

For the Ceremony

Chuppa.com • *Wedding canopy for Jewish weddings*

EarthlyPursuits.com • *Meanings of flowers*

JudaicaEMB.com • *Custom kippahs for Jewish weddings*

OriginalRunners.com • *Custom aisle runners*

PipeBand.com • *Bagpipe band locator*

SpiritualHumanism.org • *Ordain an officiant*

ULC.org • *Ordain an officiant*

WorldWeddingTraditions.com • *Ethnic and cultural traditions*

For the Reception

BBJLinen.com • *Table setting and linen resource + ideas*

ChairCovers.net • *Chair cover and table linen resource + ideas*

ClothConnection.com • *Chair cover and table linen resource + ideas*

ConfettiCakes.com • *Wedding cake ideas*

CustomLovesongs.com • *Create a custom love song*

PerfecTune.com • *Create a custom love song*

PhotoworksInteractive.com • *Photo booth rentals for events*

RentalHQ.com • *Table, chair and tent rental resource*

SouleMusic.com • *Create unique music to walk down the aisle to*

Keepsakes & Preservation

GownCare.com • *Wedding gown preservation resource*

HellerandreID.com • *Bouquet preservation service*

The Bridal Party

Bridesmaid.com · *Ideas, resources and information*
Bridesmaid101.com · *Information and resources for bridesmaids*
DiamondReview.com · *Diamond buying guide*
Gem.net · *Information on gems, shapes and cuts*
InstantWeddingToasts.com · *Create a toast*
Perfect-Bridesmaids-Dresses.com · *Bridesmaids dress resource*
SarnoTux.com/glossary.asp · *Glossary of tuxedo terms*
TheBestMan.com · *Information and resources for best man*
ThePerfectToast.com · *Create a toast*
Tie-a-tie.net/bowtie.html · *How to tie a bowtie*
Wikipedia.org/wiki/black_tie · *Tuxedo styles and traditions*

Spreading the Word

JanBoyd.com · *Calligraphy resource*
Shutterfly.com · *Post your wedding photos*
Snapfish.com · *Post your wedding photos*
SnappyMap.com · *Create a map for your guests*
StylishAddressing.com · *Calligraphy resource*
Verseit.com · *What to say and etiquette*
Wedding.orders.com · *Invitation resourse*

Vendors Resources

Adja.org · *Disc jockey resource*
DiscJockeys.com · *Disc jkockey resource*
GigMaster.com · *Music and entertainment resource*
Limos.com · *Locate a local limo company*
WedAlert.com · *Wedding music library*
WeddingMusicUSA.com · *Music and entertainment resource*
WeddingPhotoUSA.com · *Wedding photographer resource*
WeDJ.com · *Disc jockey resource*

Related Events

101BachelorettePartytips.com · *Bachelorette party resource*
HoneymoonLocation.com · *Honeymoon destination ideas*
TheHoneymoon.com · *Honeymoon planning and destination ideas*

Timeline

Although the number of tasks ahead of you seem infinite, there is actually an end to them out there, somewhere, and we found it. Follow this timeline from the moment you say I do, and everything should come off without a hitch—rather, with only the one particular hitch you're hoping for.

First Thing
- ◎ Announce your engagement
- ◎ Appraise and insure your engagement ring

9-12 Months to Go
- ◎ Hire wedding planner if desired
- ◎ Determine size, locations of ceremony and reception
- ◎ Set the date
- ◎ Decide your wedding style
- ◎ Set budget
- ◎ Select attendants
- ◎ Interview and schedule the officiant
- ◎ Create a guest list
- ◎ Shop for the gown
- ◎ Register for gifts
- ◎ Have engagement party
- ◎ Create a wedding web page

6-9 Months to Go
- ◎ Book caterer
- ◎ Order gown and schedule fittings
- ◎ Purchase shoes, headpiece, veil, jewelry and bridal lingerie
- ◎ Select the bridesmaids' dresses
- ◎ Select and book photographer and videographer
- ◎ Select and book florist
- ◎ Select and book musicians and entertainment
- ◎ Start planning the honeymoon
- ◎ Send out save-the-date cards

4-6 Months to Go
◎ Select and order all wedding stationery
◎ Book a calligrapher
◎ Check out bakeries for wedding cake
◎ Select and schedule wedding day transportation
◎ Compile a wedding shower guest list
◎ Reserve and book bridal suite and accommodations for out-of-town guests
◎ Book honeymoon trip
◎ Plan rehearsal dinner and morning after brunch and reserve locations
◎ Reserve equipment rentals
◎ Select and purchase wedding bands
◎ Select the groom's attire
◎ Select the groomsmen's attire
◎ Sign up for dance lessons
◎ Choose table favors
◎ Select and purchase wedding party gifts

2-4 Months to Go
◎ Select and order flower girl dress and ring bearer suit
◎ Apply for marriage license
◎ Buy and wrap shower, rehearsal dinner, morning-after brunch hostess gifts
◎ Shop for outfits for showers, rehearsal dinner, morning-after brunch
◎ Order rehearsal dinner and morning-after brunch invitations
◎ Plan food tasting sessions with your caterer and bakery
◎ Meet with officiant to discuss wedding ceremony thoughts and ideas
◎ Schedule time and date of rehearsal
◎ Write your vows
◎ Select ceremony and reception music
◎ Order or create welcome baskets
◎ Have wedding bands engraved
◎ Make table linen selection
◎ Finalize menu
◎ Try hair and make up
◎ Mail invitations
◎ Create wedding countdown schedule for family and friends
◎ Update passports if necessary

4-8 Weeks to Go

◎ Purchase guest book, toasting glasses, cake knife, ring pillow, flower girl basket, wedding cameras and other traditional wedding accoutrements
◎ Have programs printed
◎ Register for a marriage license
◎ Change insurance policies
◎ Set up joint bank accounts
◎ Get blood tests
◎ Submit change of address to post office
◎ Arrange and sign prenuptial agreement
◎ Send wedding announcements to local newspapers
◎ Submit name change application
◎ Change name on passport
◎ Change name on social security card
◎ Change name on driver's license
◎ Schedule final floral meeting
◎ Select and purchase wedding gifts for each other

2-4 Weeks to Go

◎ Create seating chart
◎ Contact and confirm details with all vendors
◎ Give photographer list of must-get photos
◎ Give videographer list of must-get interviews
◎ Schedule final fitting with lingerie and shoes; hair, nails, makeup, wax and all other pre-wedding appointments
◎ Do trial runs with hair stylist and makeup artist
◎ Final alterations for groom's attire
◎ Call all guests who have not replied
◎ Finalize guest list and send to calligrapher for place cards
◎ Finalize your vows
◎ Finalize your toast
◎ Wrap bridal party gifts (to distribute between now and rehearsal dinner)

1 Week to Go

- ◎ Create a final wedding and event schedule and distribute to bridal party, family and out-of-town guests
- ◎ Final fitting and arrange for delivery of gown
- ◎ Pick up and press groomsmen attire
- ◎ All attendants should have their attire ready and in hand
- ◎ Pick up place cards, table numbers, programs, etc.
- ◎ Deliver a final head count to caterer or hotel
- ◎ Pack for honeymoon
- ◎ Arrange for someone to take home bride and groom's attire, keepsakes, gifts and other items
- ◎ Deliver out-of-town gift baskets
- ◎ Deliver favors to venue
- ◎ Put together wedding emergency kit
- ◎ Reconfirm honeymoon plans and finalize itinerary

The Day Before

- ◎ Confirm transportation arrangements
- ◎ Rehearsal and rehearsal dinner
- ◎ Prepare payment and tips for vendors and officiant and arrange for someone to distribute them
- ◎ Manicure and pedicure
- ◎ Finalize wedding day schedule and assignments
- ◎ Get a massage, eat a fine meal and hopefully get a good night's sleep

Wedding Day

- ◎ Hair and makeup
- ◎ Bring emergency kit
- ◎ Bring contact information for all of your vendors
- ◎ Make sure to eat and drink water
- ◎ Say, "I do."

NOTES:

_____

_____

_____

_____

_____

_____

_____

_____

_____

_____

_____

_____

_____

_____

_____

_____

_____

_____

_____

_____

_____

Wedding Shops

Those hefty wedding magazines you've run out to buy will serve two purposes as you plan your big day. First, as you carry them around and rip out pages you like, they will help develop your upper body strength. Second, they will give you an idea about the sort of products you like, while providing examples of decorating schemes to show your vendors. However, tracking down the items you see in the magazine may prove difficult in the real world. Online, it's another story.

The internet houses more favors, decorations, invitations, keepsakes, accessories and apparel than you would ever want to view. Nevertheless, the thorough bride will revel in the mighty selection afforded by the web shops in the following pages. The less finicky bride will be able to find suitable items with ease when she uses our indexes, key words or iconography. The great advantage here is that each will be able to purchase anything she sees, on the spot. Ultimately, we'd recommend shopping around at least a little bit, because every link on every one of these web sites will potentially lead you to a page of products better than the last. Does perfection exist? That's impossible to say. All we know is that, when it comes to planning your wedding, the internet will get you close, and this book will tell you how to do it.

A wedding itself is one of the most wonderful and anticipated traditions in our lives, no matter what heritage, origin or religion we claim. Incorporating what you believe in or elements of faith or where you come from only enrich and enhance the experience. Many cultures and religions have specific rituals and traditions that they follow during the marriage ceremony, from jumping a broom to breaking a glass. For the purposes of this book, it would take too long to mention them all; suffice it to say that you should look to your family heritage, background and beliefs to make your wedding day meaningful. Whether you light a unity candle, stand under a chuppah, or have bagpipes playing, customs enrich the entire experience.

There are a few traditions that seem to have become universal to most American wedding ceremonies, so lets talk about those. The rhyme "Something old, something new, something borrowed, something blue, and a silver sixpence in your shoe" actually dates back to the Victorian era, but the customs it incorporates are much older and pulled from different cultures. However, the symbolism and meaning still rings true and is appropriate for weddings today.

Something old: Continuity
Something new: Optimism and hope
Something borrowed: Happiness shared by a married couple
Something blue: Fidelity, love, purity and luck
Sixpence for her shoe: Ensures a life of good fortune

Some of the other elements we have come to expect include the garter toss, cutting of the cake, tossing of the bouquet, and the throwing of rice or rose petals. They all serve to ritualize one of the most special days of our lives, creating lasting memories and connecting us to history.

>> Using the Book

thepurplebook
REQUIREMENTS & STANDARDS

Finding just any online retailer is easy. Finding the good ones—that takes a bit of work. We've scoured search engines, message boards, magazines and web directories in search of great sites, and received recommendations from our readers and friends. Tens of thousands of web sites promised the best prices and the greatest selections, but we took a close look at each one, and held them up to the following list of requirements:

SECURE TRANSACTIONS

Each site must offer a secure credit card transaction that can be completed in a single session. This means we disqualified any sites that only accept fax orders, email inquiries, payments over the phone or PayPal transactions. These methods of payment are both less secure and less reliable than those for sites operating encrypted commerce engines.

CUSTOMER SERVICE NUMBER

Every site in thepurplebook must provide a working customer service number. Finding this number is not always easy, and in some cases we've had to play detective to get it, but we've included one with each site listed in this book, because we've found that a lack of direct contact with a service representative can ruin an otherwise satisfactory shopping experience.

OPEN BROWSING

No site will be listed in thepurplebook that requires consumers to enter credit card numbers or other personal data before viewing its full catalog of products. Such sites usually intend to sell a customer's personal information for profit.

If an e-tailor met these requirements, we then subjected it to our own rigorous set of standards, scrutinizing each aspect of the site: Is it easy to use? Does it have a good selection? Are the prices good? Will it download in a reasonable amount of time? We whittled down the selection to include only the finest catalogs, the most beautiful web designs, the best bargains and that occasional ingenious purveyor of a product or service of such unique charm that we couldn't possibly leave it out. Our final tally includes brick-and-mortar stores that have established a viable online presence, manufacturers who have done the same, internet juggernauts that have managed to survive the dot-com backlash and small businesses, often individuals working out of their bedrooms, who've embraced the virtual marketplace in their pursuit of the American dream. It's a pretty good bunch, capable of fulfilling nearly any online shopping need you may have, and possibly turning you on to something new.

thepurplebook
ONLINE SHOPPING FUNDAMENTALS

Make a habit of using these tips and precautions, and your online shopping experience will be easy, convenient, fruitful and, above all, safe.

USE ONE CREDIT CARD
Dedicate a single credit card for all of your online purchases. This makes it especially easy to spot fraudulent and/or unauthorized charges.

PRINT A COPY
To document your online purchases, print a copy of both your order page (before you click the Submit button) and your order confirmation (receipt) to save for your records.

SAVE ALL CORRESPONDENCE
Online retailers should email a confirmation of your order and/or shipping information. Save these emails until you are fully satisfied with your purchase, as you may need to refer to this information if problems arise.

PROTECT YOURSELF AGAINST IDENTITY THEFT
Never give out credit card numbers or any personal information via email. Emails are not secure, and identity thieves commonly pose as customer service representatives in order to acquire your payment information. Only submit personal data through a secure, encrypted web site.

REPORT FRAUD IMMEDIATELY
If you suspect fraud or other mistakes, notify your credit card company and/or the Federal Trade Commission (877-382-4357) immediately, because identity thieves will not waste any time abusing your information.

USE THE CUSTOMER SERVICE NUMBER
thepurplebook has provided a customer service phone number for every shopping site listed in the book. Do not hesitate to use them. If you have any question not addressed by the web site, speak to a customer service representative before placing an order (you may be required to call during normal business hours).

USE THE COMMENTS BOX
Most online order forms offer a comments box for special requests or any questions you may have. This will be the surest way of contacting the actual humans in charge of fulfilling your order, so that they can properly address your needs.

READ THE WEB SITE'S POLICIES
Before you make a purchase, take note of the web site's return and exchange policies, as well as shipping, privacy and security, because once you place your order, you've agreed to their terms and conditions. The FAQ (Frequently Asked Questions) section of a web site often proves a good source of information.

AVOID UNWANTED SOLICITATIONS
When entering your billing and email address, a lot of shopping sites will ask if you're interested in receiving catalogs and/or advertising materials from them and other sites. In most cases, the answer defaults to *Yes*, and you'll need to actively change this answer to *No* if you hope to avoid junk mail and spam.

REPORT BAD BUSINESS PRACTICES
If you do have a bad experience with an online retailer, make a report to the Better Business Bureau, at BBB.org.

>> Useful Resources

The following URLs may be useful when you shop online.

BBB.org • *Better Business Bureau site*

Consumer.gov/idtheft • *Identity theft information and warnings*

ConsumerReports.org • *Consumer product reviews*

CountryCallingCodes.com • *International country calling codes*

CPSC.gov • *Product recall lists*

CreditCardGuide.org • *Credit card information*

EquiFax.com • *Obtain your credit report*

Experian.com • *Obtain your credit report*

KidStockMontana.com/sizing.html • *Clothes sizing charts*

LittleShoes.com • *Shoes and clothes sizing charts*

MyUS.com • *Forward packages to overseas addresses*

NetLingo.com • *Glossary of internet terms*

OAndA.com • *Currency converter*

ShopForDSL.com • *Compare local internet service providers*

SmartQpon.com • *Coupon codes for online retailers*

TransUnion.com • *Obtain your credit report*

WhatsItWorthToYou.com • *Online appraisals*

NOTES:

_____

_____

_____

_____

_____

_____

_____

_____

_____

_____

_____

_____

_____

_____

_____

_____

_____

_____

_____

≫ Go Shopping!

HOW TO USE thepurplebook

While we've made every effort to be discriminating, the number of web sites listed in this book does exceed 300. Though these comprise a mere fraction of the thousands of sites we viewed, we're well aware that it's a lot to handle. If you're looking for a good place to shop or find a gift, you can browse the alphabetical site listings. If you have something more specific in mind, you can search one of our several indexes for products, companies or key words.

�֎ BROWSING

thepurplebook wedding site listings are arranged alphabetically by URL and presented along with a five-or-six-line review that should give you a general idea of what to expect from the site before ever logging on. Alongside these reviews, you will find icons that evaluate the site's service, selection and usability, as well as a list of key words describing the store's product selection.

Using the icons and key words, you can browse each category to find specific product types, or to locate stores that offer services like gift wrapping or overnight delivery. See the sample site listing below, and the descriptions on the following pages, for further details.

Ⓑ

Nordstrom.com **Ⓐ**
888-282-6060

Ⓒ You're probably already familiar with this Seattle-based department store, and possibly even its well-rounded web site. What you may not realize is that, if you look into the Women's section, you'll find a designated Wedding Shop designed to meet the apparel and accessory needs of the bride, mother of the bride, bridesmaids and flower girls, including some lovely, affordable wedding dresses, jewelry and shoes.

Ⓓ   **Ⓔ**

APPAREL GROOM	ATTENDANTS JEWELRY	BRIDE SHOES & ACCESSORIES

Ⓕ

✳ UNDERSTANDING THE SITE LISTINGS

Ⓐ URL
Each site in this book has been listed alphabetically by its URL (internet address). We've left out the standard http://www. that precedes each domain name and extension. In other words, to visit ModernSeed.com, go to the address bar in your browser and type in http://www.modernseed.com.

Ⓑ CUSTOMER SERVICE NUMBERS
We've listed each company's customer service phone number along with its entry (some sites like to hide them). This should help if you can't log on to the site for some reason, or if you cannot find the number listed there. When things go wrong, using the web site's human support staff is often more productive than sending emails.

Ⓒ REVIEW
These reviews are intended to offer some insight into the breadth and scope of the web site at hand, hopefully with a little good-natured fun. After all, we've found that many of the best shopping sites have terrific senses of humor.

Ⓓ CUSTOMER SERVICE ICONS
The set of round customer service icons found throughout the book depict some of the particulars about each store that may come in handy when deciding where to shop: shipping costs, overnight shipping, gift certificates, gift wrapping, user-friendliness, a star to indicate whether a site is exceptionally useful or unique and the word *Wish* to designate sites offering wish lists or gift registries.

Ⓔ WEDDING EDITION ICONS
The rectangular icons have been included to help you distinguish which sites will cater to your functional, decorative, fashion, non-traditional and gift-giving needs.

Ⓕ KEY WORDS
At the bottom of each site listing, you will find a list of key words that offer general descriptions of the types of products available from that site. A quick scan of these words should give you a rough idea of whether a site has what you seek.

✳ UNDERSTANDING THE ICONS

CUSTOMER SERVICE ICONS

SHIPPING COSTS

A huge consideration when shopping online is the cost of shipping and handling. High fees can turn what seemed like a great deal into a waste of cash, whereas a cheap shipping policy can mean the difference between competitive prices.

Free, Incentivized or Flat Rate Shipping – Sites marked by this icon either cover shipping costs, reduce the cost of shipping if you spend more or charge a single, preset amount to cover shipment of your entire order, regardless of cost or weight.

Standard Shipping Rates – Sites covered by this icon either charge the same weight-based amount for shipping as determined by the carrier (usually UPS, FedEx, Airborne Express, DHL or the US Postal Service), or compute comparable rates based on the value of the purchase.

Exorbitant or Unknown Shipping & Handling Fees – Sites tagged with this icon either charge excessive handling fees designed to pad their profit margins or do not inform you of an order's shipping charges until after a credit card has been used to make the purchase. A third category of these sites simply ship very large, heavy items that require special companies or even individual trucks, usually at great expense.

OVERNIGHT SHIPPING

When you see this icon, the site in question offers overnight shipping or next-day delivery, in most cases at an extra charge, and often not on weekends. Bear in mind that sites usually have an early-afternoon or morning deadline for one-day delivery, and that time zones may consequently play a big role in your last-minute purchases.

GIFT CERTIFICATES

This icon only appears when gift certificates are available for purchase, in either electronic or paper form. Electronic gift certificates will be sent to the recipient's email address, and therefore make excellent last-second gifts.

GIFT WRAPPING

Many sites listed within this book offer some pretty great gifts, and most will send your order in a plain brown box. However, some will wrap it up a bit nicer (usually at an extra charge). Such sites are noted by this icon.

USER-FRIENDLINESS

Product selection is the most important aspect to building an online store, but presentation is often what sells, and if using a site to make a purchase is just too much work it may not be worth it. We've ranked each site's performance with the following three icons:

Easy – These sites have gone the distance to make sure that you can find the products you need without hassle and order them with minimal difficulty, either through fancy web design or plain common sense. Or the site has only a handful of products to begin with and everything may be viewed or purchased on one page. Either way, we wish all the sites qualified for this rank, but very few did.

Standard – Savvy web shoppers are used to the industry standard—a left-side menu of options, with a few more general choices thrown across the top of the page for good measure. Such sites warrant no complaints, as everything you need is laid out logically so that browsing and buying is easy on the mind, and only hard on the mouse-clicking finger.

Difficult – In some cases, these sites involve failed attempts to create the virtual world's best new shopping technique. On the flipside are the purely bad web designs. Whatever the case, these sites are often impossible to load, browse and/or order from. Ironically, these aberrations wouldn't have made the cut except that they're offering some of the best the web has to offer.

WISH LISTS & REGISTRIES

This icon will clue you in to sites offering wish lists and gift registries. These will allow you to browse and save all the products you want so that your friends and loved ones may browse your selection at their leisure and buy you the perfect gift every time. This feature is particularly useful when others are helping pay for your wedding.

WEDDING SHOPS ICONS

CEREMONY & RECEPTION

 Much of your wedding planning will revolve around all the decorations, food, flowers and accessories necessary to prepare the ceremony and reception to your guests' enjoyment. Look here for favors, keepsakes and sundry traditional items.

GIFTS

 When your best friends and family take on the time, effort and expense to stand with you on your big day, they deserve a lot of credit. Offering thanks in the form of a gift is customary, and this icon will guide you to a cornucopia of wonderful gift ideas.

DIVERSE CUSTOMS & BRIGHT IDEAS

 Traditional American weddings are well represented by the vast majority of sites we've discovered. However, as there are plenty of different cultural customs and personal preferences, we've provided this icon to highlight those shops catering to those who aren't planning on the usual.

PERSONALIZATION

 The personalized products we've found online include stationery, gifts, jewelry, keepsakes, favors, hankerchiefs, ribbons, apparel and even cake toppers. Watch out for this icon to find something you can put anybody's name to.

PLANNING & PAPERWORK

 There's a lot you'll need to consider well in advance of your wedding, the first of which is engagement announcments. Following that we have save-the-date cards, invitations, bridal showers, bachlor parties and less fun stuff like name change documents and marriage licenses. Find planning assistance with this icon.

THE WEDDING PARTY

 Everybody involved in your ceremony will need clothes, shoes and various other accessories. From the bride and groom right on down to the ring bearer, flower girl and other attendants, check for this icon to locate every necessary accoutrement to outfit your dream wedding.

✳ KEY WORD DEFINITIONS

APPAREL
It's simple enough; this key word denotes the clothing worn by members of the bridal party, be it bridal gowns, tuxedos, bridesmaid dresses, flower girl dresses or less formal attire.

ATTENDANTS
Each member of the bridal party may be referred to by this word, from the maid of honor and best man to the ring bearer and mother of the bride. You'll see it used in reference to apparel as well as to gifts, shoes and accessories.

BRIDE
This most important key word will guide you directly to those shops that cater to the bride's trousseau, including gowns, lingerie, jewelry, headpieces, shoes, gloves, hats and handbags.

DIY
Since many wedding shops recognize the financial need and creative desire for some brides to make some of their own invitations, programs, favors, accessories, cakes and centerpieces, we've highlighted them with this do-it-yourself key word.

DOCUMENTATION
There are many kinds of documents associated with getting married, not the least of which is the marriage license. However, there are also name change forms to be considered, and other matters of record, including photographs, with cameras often available where you find this word.

FAVORS & DECOR
This key word covers a lot of ground, ranging from ribbons and party lights to sparklers and bubbles, any party favor or decorative touch that might improve your ceremony or reception. As it turns out, most sites represented by this word also cover a lot of ground.

FLOWERS
Probably no key word is easier to figure out than this one. However, we should point out that along with floral arrangements, bouquets, corsages, boutonnieres and petals, we've used this word to indicate fake flowers, bouquets and petals.

FOOD

Whether you're serving appetizers, candy or cake, many of the sites within this book can help make your reception much more delicious. Just look for this key word.

GROOM

The groom doesn't typically take as active an interest in the sundry decorative and stylish touches involved in planning a wedding, but that doesn't mean we haven't thought about him here. This word leads to suits, tuxedos, cufflinks, dress shoes and the like, and since his best man and groomsmen usually wear the same sort of stuff, it may refer to them as well.

JEWELRY

The term *jewelry* is fairly self-explanatory, and there's some pretty important jewelry invovled in any wedding. Here, we've included engagement rings and wedding bands; however, we may also be referring to bridal jewelry or baubles intended as bridesmaid gifts.

KEEPSAKES

These are the lovely little souvenirs meant to remind you of this finest of days. Common keepsakes include tussie-mussies, wedding cake charms, cake toppers, toasting flutes, guest books, wedding albums and handkerchiefs. Many can be personalized.

PARTIES & SHOWERS

The fun starts long before you walk down the aisle, and if your best man or maid of honor needs a little help throwing you a shower or bachelor/bachelorette party, send them looking for this key word, where they'll find games, decor and possibly a cigar or two.

SHOES & ACCESSORIES

The shoes referred to here are a no-brainer. Accessories, on the other hand, may cover gloves, hats, handbags, hair accessories, headpieces, parasols, tiaras and more.

STATIONERY

Primarily this word will lead you to massive selections of invitations and announcements. However, you might also find programs, guest books and wedding albums. Still, you might want to use the index to find those; this word turns up a lot.

✳ USING THE INDEXES

These indexes at the end of the book will help you track down specific products, stores and sites of interest in the most efficient manner.

PRODUCT INDEX (page 184)
A detailed listing of products and the corresponding names of sites that carry them. Note that this is not necessarily a comprehensive list, and that you will be able to find some of these products on sites not mentioned in the index.

KEY WORD INDEXES (page 198)
A key word index that can help you locate which stores carry particular types of products within that general category.

COMPANY INDEX (page 214)
This list of brand and company names is simply meant to help you find web sites for companies that may not otherwise be familiar.

FIND ONLY WHAT YOU NEED... AND LET US KNOW WHAT YOU LIKE
We at thepurplebook are always looking for ways to improve this book, and we welcome all constructive criticism, suggestions and feedback. Visit us at thepurplebook.com for more information.

1800Flowers.com 800-468-1141

Nothing gets a chance to stand out on this very busy and colorful site, but if you can track down the Wedding Flowers and Gifts link, you'll quickly spot a lovely assortment of bouquets, corsages, boutonnieres and table centerpieces. The selection here is small, but that's no matter since the rest of the massive site happens to feature an incredibly wide variety of floral arrangements, and there's sure to be something here to match your bridal tastes.

BRIDE	FAVORS & DECOR	FLOWERS

4YourParty.com 877-228-3701

Setting up an informal reception is easy with this site, despite the difficulties you may have navigating its clunky menu. Paper and plastic plates, forks, napkins, tablecloths and stemware offer very affordable serving options as well as quick cleanup opportunities (straight into the recycling bin). It's definitely something to consider if you're on a tight budget, or if you're just not the crystal and fine china type.

FAVORS & DECOR		

5Inch.com 773-862-0291

Personal devices that play MP3s and video files may have pushed CDs and DVDs out of your mind for a while, but this blank media specialist is likely to push them right back. Rather than offer blank discs with the name of some giant corporation printed across the top, this shop offers an assortment of CD-Rs in a variety of colors that are just as blank across the top. Better yet, you may opt for discs with cool silkscreen-printed designs, or even custom order media with your own illustrations printed across the top. Whether you wish to hand these out to your guests as favors or send audio/video thank-you notes, this site can't be beat.

DIY	FAVORS & DECOR	

800-603-9940   **Abazias.com**

As of this writing, this diamond ring specialist offered "85,400 diamonds and 93,582 carats," which of course can be a lot to sort through, even presuming you're incredibly excited about your engagement ring. Fortunately, the site offers an excellent, user-friendly search technique that allows you to adjust your diamond search by the stone's shape, price and carat range, then further adjust for clarity and color. This proves important as you use the Ring Builder feature to piece together the perfect ring, then view your creation in 3D before you buy.

BRIDE	JEWELRY	

877-822-7672   **AbsorbCreative.com**

There are many invitations and announcements shops out there, and few of them really stand out. Consequently, not too many invitations stand out, either. This stationer has solved that problem by offering to incorporate your own photograph into the cards. Not only will this ensure your invited guests remember just whose nuptials they'll be attending, but if you select the right, sweet photo of the happy couple, they'll be more inclined to attend, and not just for the free meal.

STATIONERY		

011-32-3-213-65-00   **Adin.be**

Among Western European nations, Belgium is easy to overlook when it comes to high fashion. However, this fantastic estate jewelry retailer reminds us not only that the lowland country exists, but that it's worth noticing. In particular, some very special engagement rings exist here in abundance and will blow your mind. As it happens, any specific type of piece you're looking for, from cufflinks to pearls, should be easy to find, as the site's browsing filters let you wade through a potentially complicated assortment of fine vintage jewelry without much hassle.

BRIDE	GROOM	JEWELRY

AdvantageBridal.com   877-933-7467

If you're ready to be overwhelmed by the sheer volume of wedding products available on this planet, this supersite will prove a complicated but terrific place to start. Favorable shipping rates makes it worthwhile to get any and all of the following available items: personalized wedding party gifts, table settings, tiaras, keepsakes, name change kits, music, shoes, dresses, flower baskets, ring pillows, cake toppers and more. So much more it would take a full page to explain.

ATTENDANTS JEWELRY	DOCUMENT KEEPSAKES	FAVORS & DECOR SHOES & ACCESSORIES

AgentProvocateur.com   44-0-870-727-4169

You have plenty of options when it comes to spicing up the honeymoon with sexy lingerie, but this British brand may provide your best one. Elegant and classic, the Bridal line incorporates white corsets and garters, along with a gorgeous selection of bras, demi-bras, quarter bras and several varieties of lace panties. You may also want to browse other available sets, such as Kabaret, Bunny and Calamity, because by the second or third night, even a newlywed can appreciate red or black lingerie.

APPAREL	BRIDE	

Alight.com   516-367-1095

Sizes 14 to 28w will probably not do better than to check out the selection of this all-encompassing women's apparel site. There's loads of great, stylish stuff here—and we mean stylish: well made and good looking. It doesn't matter if you favor a modest approach to dressing, or if you embrace a tight sensuality; these clothes manage to be complimentary without being patronizing. Which is one of the things that make the site's Wedding Styles boutique a great source for bridesmaid attire.

APPAREL	ATTENDANTS	

877-727-3702   **AllysonSmith.com**

Like a Southerner transplanted to New York City, the semiprecious jewelry available from this designer's site stands out with a burst of color against cold urban gray. Which makes sense, seeing as the Louisiana-born designer in question has taken the Big Apple by storm with her bright, dazzling and especially stylish bracelets, earrings and necklaces. We wish there were more to see (there are fewer than 200 pieces here), but this is just one inspired woman with an eye for fashionable jewelry, so we suggest taking a look at the full collection, buying some as bridal jewelry and some as attendant gifts.

ATTENDANTS	BRIDE	JEWELRY

888-953-9455   **AlohaInvitations.com**

Beach or island weddings already offer your guests plenty of reasons to attend, but if you'd like to drive the point home with an original and impossible-to-ignore invitation, do not miss this site's Invitation in a Bottle service. Though more costly to mail than traditional envelopes, these bottles arrive in your guests' mailboxes containing seashells, a treasure map scroll and a tiny starfish. Beautiful as well as clever, the only way they could be better is if they actually floated in with the tide.

STATIONERY		

800-808-6276   **AmazingButterflyStore.com**

There are not a lot of insect species that will actually make a wedding better, and at the top of that very short list you find the butterfly. This surprisingly focused butterfly specialist will actually overnight ship a decorative box filled with live butterflies that will be all too eager to fly out into the open air once released. More graceful than doves, less messy than rice or confetti, this awe-inspiring alternative to the wedding toss is guaranteed to delight.

FAVORS & DECOR		

AmericanBridal.com   800-568-3398

This very well-organized site offers myriad options for wedding accessories and decor, as well as a slew of bridal party gifts. It's easy to use, too, as they've added expandable navigation menus that enable you to find every ample selection with a well-placed click. Add to that the list of wedding resources and a Shop by Price feature, and finding reception decorations, favors, bridal accessories and ceremony essentials takes just a few moments and absolutely no fuss. Other than the heavy reliance on pastels, all wedding sites would be like this if the groom planned the ceremony.

ATTENDANTS FAVORS & DECOR	DIY	DOCUMENT

AmericanStationery.com   800-822-2577

Thanks to rampant commercialism and kitschy pop culture, the words *American* and *elegant* aren't always thought of in the same context. This personalized stationery site is happy to disagree, offering fine and sophisticated letterheads, cards and paper at good, old-fashioned, affordable American prices. Whether you prefer embossed letterheads or decorative hand-drawn borders, the site offers a lovely selection that maintains the same great taste the shop has shown for more than eighty-five years. In other words, good taste that predates television.

STATIONERY		

Anandia.com   949-200-7526

As "diamonds of the sea," pearls are said to "transcend trends, suit every mood, and are perfect for every occasion." At least, that's what the purveyors of this site say, and they should know: pearls are their business. The Newport Beach, California, retailer offers a gorgeous array of pearl necklaces, bracelets, earrings and more, and what could be better adornments for a beautiful, white-clad bride than the sea-born stones revered throughout history as "drops of moonlight?"

ATTENDANTS	BRIDE	JEWELRY

011-39-055-284-977   Anichini.net

This oldest children's clothing store in Florence, Italy, offers a fine selection of traditional European styles for boys, girls, and babies who prefer the more refined and venerable look of a young aristocrat on the make. Available in a variety of high-quality fabrics and colors, these ceremonial baby gowns and fine-tailored dress clothes should probably not be left on your flower girl or ring bearer unsupervised; given the high cost and lengthy delivery process, these aren't clothes you want to sacrifice to your kids' attraction to dirt.

APPAREL	ATTENDANTS	

800-821-7011   AnnsWedding.com

Your thematic wedding can be off to a solid start with this stationery retailer specializing in topical invitations. Follow the Wedding Invitations link from the home page, then click on Refine Search to wade through categories such as Fairy-Tale, Doves, Western and Traditional styles. You may also search using budget and color considerations, and though you won't find a vast array of choices, most should be appropriate to your wedding theme and, once you've selected among the various typesetting options, will possess the air of personal preference.

STATIONERY			

800-342-5266   AnnTaylor.com

Fans of Ann Taylor will definitely appreciate this site, especially those selected to be a bridesmaid. Although the entire site is worth an afternoon's worth of browsing, if you follow the Celebrations link in the Apparel menu you'll find a very small but beautiful assortment of dresses, tops and skirts. These are lovely enough that a woman may even want to wear them once all of her ceremonial obligations are complete. In other words, you won't find any pink taffeta here.

APPAREL	ATTENDANTS	

AntiqueAndEstate.com888-656-765

Billing itself as "Your source for one of a kind jewelry," this site runs a real risk of setting your expectations too high. Except this unique antique and estate jewelry selection is fine, beautiful and constantly changing, and we dare you to be disappointed. Probably the best place to shop for an engagement ring for that girl with vintage tastes (you'll need to have it resized locally), and wedding bands beyond the pale. Happy hunting!

BRIDE	GROOM	JEWELRY

AntiqueJewelryExch.com800-809-419

Jewelry is a very popular family heirloom, which generally means that the best jewelry gets handed down through the generations and never again sees the light of a marketplace. Appropriate, then, that this family owned-and-operated business is one that specifically seeks out antique and estate jewels, to create one of the richer and finer jewelry selections online. Specializing in platinum, they certainly have lovely items to display in several categories, but in particular some of the engagement rings retain a character and charm seldom seen in contemporary catalogs.

BRIDE	JEWELRY	

AntiqueJewelryMall.com800-292-4900

With "unique antique and estate jewelry from the Victorian, Edwardian, Art Nouveau, Art Deco, Mid-Century Retro Moderne, and contemporary periods," this massive web retailer offers a broad range of beautifully crafted pieces, but no section of the site is better than the Wedding Jewelry pages. Engagement rings and wedding bands abound, often as beautiful as they get. Of course, there's plenty of other estate jewelry available, including a deep assortment of cufflinks and plenty of pieces that would make unique attendant gifts.

ATTENDANTS JEWELRY	BRIDE	GROOM

AppetizersToGo.com
800-757-0058

If you decide to cater your own wedding, you'll have to face down the many daunting tasks that cooking for large groups of people entails. This site can do a lot to ease your burden, though—at least part of it. The first part. With an extraordinary selection of appetizing heat-and-serve hors d'oeuvres to choose from, you can offer your guests a wide variety of dumplings, cheese puffs, stuffed mushrooms, mini quiches, buffalo wings, chicken fingers, crab cakes and rangoons. Prepare enough and you won't even need to worry about the main course.

DIY | FOOD

AsianIdeas.com
888-384-3327

When the search for wedding planning inspiration brings you to this site, you'll find "thousands of years of Asian history and culture" at your disposal. How many shops can promise that? A lovely selection of products covers a wide range of categories, but if you pay keen attention to the Tableware and Party Supplies sections, you'll come across beautiful paper lanterns, parasols, table settings, favor boxes and other splendid decorative touches your guest will adore.

FAVORS & DECOR

Bachelorette.com
800-809-0610

If you are the bride-to-be, you might not want to look too close at this site, or you might start to fear your own bachelorette party. All the costuming, games, candies, decorations and favors offer a rare glimpse into just how rowdy and deviant a group of gals can get when they're sending off one of their own. The groom, especially, should work hard to avoid getting a glimpse of anything but the Bachelor Party section; and even that seems almost tame by comparison. Don't worry, though; the shop offers plenty of tasteful, even sweet party supplies, so you may feel free to tell your friends about it.

FAVORS & DECOR | PARTIES | STATIONERY

BachelorettePartyShop.com   847-622-4317

Just when we thought there was no altruism left in online retail, we come to this site, which was "founded back in 1998 when the owners decided that the women of this world needed a place to purchase hilarious bachelorette party items." Featuring a variety of party games, gag gifts, favors and decorations, this stuff ranges from the risqué to the ridiculous, and we will tastefully neglect to mention anything in particular here. Actually, truth be known, there's not even anything tasteful in the Food & Drink section.

FAVORS & DECOR	PARTIES	STATIONERY

BacheloretteSuperstore.com   360-254-6505

Just how much girls-night-out humor can be derived from phallic objects? This bachelorette party specialist aims to find out, with wind-ups, inflatables, straws, candies, cake pans, cookie cutters, serving trays and a fun little game called Pin the Hose on the Fireman. It's not all so raunchy here, though, as there are plenty of games, favors and decorations that are all in good fun, as well as in good taste. All the same, you might want to pick up a few copies of the Oath to Secrecy.

FAVORS & DECOR	FOOD	PARTIES

BarriePace.com   800-441-6011

With a stylish selection of fine women's suits and career separates for regular, plus and petite sizes, this site makes a great staple for the female professional of any age. More importantly, a lovely range of sophisticated active wear and some killer cocktail dresses manage to straddle the line between sexy and refined, making it a perfect spot to shop for the bride or groom's mother, whether you shop from the label's Mother of the Bride collection, or opt for some of the aforementioned fineries.

APPAREL	ATTENDANTS	

Beau-Coup.com
877-988-2328

It's not easy to describe this wedding favor and place setting site, except to say that they offer, well, favors and place settings. Some of the favors are scented, some are silver and yet others suit specific themes, like Asian, Beach/Nautical or Sports. Still others are neither thematic, scented or silver, but can be personalized. Some of the place card holders double as favors, and other favors double as place setting decorations. With pages upon pages of items covering a broad range of interconnected categories, this is definitely one for brides-to-be who love to browse.

FAVORS & DECOR PARTIES	FOOD	KEEPSAKES

BellaBluMaternity.com
888-678-0034

With a deep selection of fun, contemporary maternity clothes, including one of the biggest swimwear selections we've seen, this online boutique comes to the web as a labor of love and it shows. The incredibly rich clearance selections will grab your attention, but you'll still want to delve into the fresher formal dresses to outfit the well-rounded belly of your pregnant bridesmaid. Choose wisely, and maybe she'll lend it to you when you start having children.

APPAREL	ATTENDANTS	

BellaRegalo.com
877-337-5996

In planning a wedding, some opt for a modern flair, while others choose to stay close to elegant tradition; this site walks the fine line between. Not nearly as starched and bland as strictly traditional favors, accessories and place settings can often be, these items nevertheless adhere to a classical aesthetic (in other words, they never get too funky). We found a great assortment of confections, including themed petit fours, strawberries dressed in chocolate wedding gowns/tuxedos and ring pillows shaped like starfish and nautical shells.

FAVORS & DECOR	FOOD	PARTIES

BellaTerra.net 626-792-4714

Contemporary and slick, this site offers products that are the same, whether personalized wedding favors or hip invitations. Some beautifully packaged seeds for the wedding toss head up the favors, followed by custom CD sleeves, matchboxes, soaps and scent-filled pouches. Even if none of the favors appeal to you, several great packaging options might, as you can buy pretty boxes, pockets and labels to be filled with whatever you like. If you're thinking ahead, you may even be able to coordinate the look of your packaging with similar invitations, which are also available to prove that you, too, are contemporary and slick.

DIY	DOCUMENT	FAVORS & DECOR

BenSilver.com 800-221-4671

Follow the Shopping link of this site and you'll be convinced it's an upscale British tailor. In truth, this clothier is headquartered in Charleston, South Carolina. Not that elegant men's apparel is the exclusive realm of London shops; we're just not used to seeing it done so fine and proper on this side of the Atlantic. In the past couple of years, the site has improved in design along with some of the three-piece suits, silk ties and tuxedos, so it's easier than ever to track down the groom's all-important accoutrements: cufflinks, pocket squares and shoes.

APPAREL SHOES & ACCESSORIES	GROOM	JEWELRY

Beryls.com 703-256-6951

When it comes to baking a wedding cake, most of us have a difficult enough time even knowing where to begin. So, for the novice baker, or even those with the right amount of know-how: this is where you begin. Not that the site goes out of its way to make it easy—browsing its many circuitous pop-up pages can start you down a complicated road. However, helpful books are available, as are cake pans, cake stands, decorations and airbrushing tools to make that elegant cake your own.

DIY	FOOD	

866-623-7765   **BespokeBoxes.com**

According to this purveyor of gift boxes, the object of giving is "to make your recipient believe that you spent a lot of time and thought on the gift, regardless of whether you actually did." Granted, if they've seen these elegant and beautifully packaged gift baskets, the jig is up, and your recipient will know you merely had to browse for two minutes on this easy-to-use site. However, if you follow the Create Your Own link, you'll rest secure in the knowledge that you at least put some work into it.

ATTENDANTS	GROOM	

8787-274-3321   **BestBridalPrices.com**

Here's a family-owned-and-operated bridal boutique out of the Midwest that offers a huge selection of dresses for the bride, bridesmaid and flower girl, always at a reasonable price. Although the site features pages upon pages of gowns by labels such as Mori Lee, Jacqueline, Amelie and Christina Wu, you might wish to check the In Stock Gowns first, where you may search by size, which ranges from 4 to 28. Of course, if you're ordering in advance, this shop will get you good prices on anything you find here, and there's plenty to like.

APPAREL SHOES & ACCESSORIES	ATTENDANTS	BRIDE

888-217-5655   **BestBridesmaid.com**

Let's face it: the perfect wedding gown is probably the single most important part of any wedding, so you don't really want to waste any of your precious time trying to find the proper dresses for your bridesmaids. This site offers a couple dozen simple and elegant dress designs for your ladies in waiting, in a variety of colors, all on one page. It adds up to be one of the quickest, easiest shopping selections you'll find anywhere, despite a lack of alternate color samples and the fact that delivery may take more than two months. The bottom line is that you'll want to order well ahead of time, in consideration of alterations.

APPAREL	ATTENDANTS	

BigFireWorks.com   888-740-1040

This one comes with a warning: even if your state allows the sale of internet fireworks, you should make sure A) that no children get hold of them and B) that only a trained professional operates these explosive materials—or at least don't let your drunk uncle do it. Now, the site's nothing special in look or flow, and the product's pretty straightforward: mostly sparklers. The only thing left to say is that hopefully the bride and groom will provide their own fireworks; otherwise, these will do.

FAVORS & DECOR		

Bissingers.com   800-325-8881

We have to warn you: this site may induce uncontrollable drooling with talk of "luscious chocolate-covered fresh fruits, decadent truffles and hand-crafted chocolate confections." If you think that's bad, wait until you see the pictures of rich, smooth chocolate as it embraces a glistening strawberry, or molded perfectly around a candied pecan. If you have this reaction just viewing the web site, imagine how your wedding guests will react to find these treats as sumptuous wedding favors....

FAVORS & DECOR	FOOD	

BlissWeddingsMarket.com   516-364-4086

The retail arm of an online magazine, the proprietors of this site vaunt a creative approach to nuptial events, stating, "more engaged couples than ever realize that their wedding day is not only a rite of passage but also a public expression of their personality as a couple." Hence, they advocate a selective reinterpretation of customs, picking out the best parts and discarding the rest. To this end, the magazine offers plenty of ideas and·guidelines, whereas a thoroughly stocked catalog includes unique and stylish favors, stationery (including labels) and bridal accessories, without veering too far from the classy course of tradition.

ATTENDANTS STATIONERY	DIY	FAVORS & DECOR

702-269-7681   **Blonde-Designs.com**

With a "shared vision of simple clean lines, soft textures and inspired imagery that celebrate life's most special occasions and milestones," the blondes behind this line of stationery left the Martha Stewart empire to create the elegant invitations, announcements and thank-you cards found here. You won't see a great deal of variety, but any of the available options are bound to elicit gushing kudos from your friends and family, and will let them know your wedding is to be a sophisticated fete indeed.

| STATIONERY | | |

877-258-3359   **BlueFly.com**

Whatever Blue Fly means is not important. What's important is that this site is an online outlet store, and that means that whatever you see here will be cheaper than it should be. Why? Who cares? Whether you're shopping for designer bridesmaid dresses or fine suits for the groom and his best men, this upscale overstock shop can make your party look sophisticated and gorgeous in labels like Gucci, Marc Jacobs, Vera Wang and Christian Dior. It's not exactly cheap, but definitely a bargain.

| APPAREL SHOES & ACCESSORIES | ATTENDANTS | GROOM |

800-242-2728   **BlueNile.com**

With a huge selection of gemstones and precious metals woven into some dazzling pieces, as well as some less expensive fashionable jewelry and watches, this site has just about all of your jewelry needs covered, and finding them is unsettlingly easy. You'll especially like the wedding bands, bridal jewelry and sparkling engagement rings, including some options you can build yourself. With financing and insurance available, you may find it hard to leave this one without making a purchase.

| BRIDE | GROOM | JEWELRY |

BlueTuxShoes.com 312-563-1858

Like us, you probably saw the name of this site and assumed it sold men's dress shoes; something snazzy to match a tuxedo. Sadly, this is not the case. On the other hand, if you're a bridesmaid, the happy truth is this small line of footwear offers dyeable and metallic shoes for the women behind the lady-of-the-hour. It couldn't be simpler to view the entire selection in less than a minute, and we suspect the hard part will be viewing it all a second time and trying to pick out a favorite pair.

ATTENDANTS	SHOES & ACCESSORIES

BotanicalPaperworks.com 877-956-7393

If you're of the do-it-yourself mentality, you'll be thrilled to find some of the out-of-the-ordinary papermaking kits available on this site. Should you have neither the time nor energy required to do this (who does, with a wedding to plan?), you can find a terrific selection of handmade invitations, guest books and even plantable favors (made by professionals, not other customers). While their ordering functionality can be a bit frustrating, with so much pretty paper (infused with petals, leaves, grasses and such), there's little else to complain about.

DIY	FAVORS & DECOR	STATIONERY

BouquetJewels.com 800-590-4970

Flowers possess a startling natural beauty and, properly arranged, will almost glow in your bridal bouquet. However, if you'd like to add a little genuine sparkle, check out this unique collection of crystals, faux diamonds and pearls, selected to adorn your floral arrangement. Set into cross, bow, butterfly and holiday shapes, or sold in loose sets that you may dress the bouquet with yourself, these shining baubles bestow an elegance only nature could ever outdo.

BRIDE JEWELRY	DIY	FLOWERS

BridalPeople.com
877-520-0259

Boasting "1000's of Bridal Necessities," this shop indeed offers a range of ceremony, reception and bridal shower accessories that includes but is not limited to: headpieces, flower girl baskets, ring bearer pillows, bridal shoes, wedding gloves, guest books, garters, money bags, cake toppers and potpourri-filled bras—you know, all of the customary favorites. Favoring elegance over attitude, this may not be the best place to shop for quirky bridal accents, but for white weddings it will more than suffice.

ATTENDANTS SHOES & ACCESSORIES	DOCUMENT STATIONERY	FAVORS & DECOR

BridalShoes.com
516-776-9225

Because a girl can never have too many choices when it comes to shoes, you'll want to check out this wedding footwear specialist. With categories devoted to boots, sandals, mid, low and high heels, perusing the many dyeable options is never difficult and, given the affordability of each pair, you might even want to pick up a couple of different styles. That way, when the big day arrives, you can make a last-minute decision about just how tall or comfortable you want to be.

ATTENDANTS	BRIDE	SHOES & ACCESSORIES

BrideSave.com
888-321-4696

In the hunt for that all-too-precious wedding gown, a woman is likely to scour every magazine, catalog and wedding album she can get her hands on, spending countless hours and viewing hundreds of dresses, the notion of perfection firm in her mind. This site, on the other hand, offers a paltry 2,600 or so to choose from. Filter by such variations as Color, Fabric, Neckline, Sleeve, Bodice, Train and/or specific Designer to get a look at several ideas, if not perfect fits to your unerring vision. With the time you save you can choose to sort through the hundreds of accessories, wedding party attire and decorations also available.

APPAREL SHOES & ACCESSORIES	ATTENDANTS	BRIDE

BrooksBrothers.com   800-556-7039

Brooks Brothers has been around for a long, long time, and has been a favorite of such far-reaching individuals as studly actor Clark Gable, boxer Jack Dempsey, pilot Charles Lindbergh and beat author Jack Kerouac. But can it outfit a wedding? With aplomb. While tuxedos will be the obvious starting point, the true value of the site may be seen in the fine suits that accommodate a ceremony with less formality but no loss in quality. Add a healthy assortment of dress shoes, ties, suspenders and cufflinks, and all your shopping for the groom, groomsmen and even ring bearers will be complete.

APPAREL SHOES & ACCESSORIES	GROOM	JEWELRY

BurdickChocolate.com   800-229-2419

If you're going to offer your wedding guests candy, consider increasing the cachet of your confections by paying a visit to this chocolatier that specializes in handmade sweets. The rich chocolates and dipped fruits would be enough on their own, but the shop goes the distance by offering a variety of personalized packaging options. With many colors to choose from, you may easily match these boxes and bags to your reception's color scheme, creating favors almost too delicious to eat.

FAVORS & DECOR	FOOD	

CakesBySam.com   800-399-6042

A more appropriate name for this site might be Cakes By You, as what it really offers is cake-making equipment and decorating ingredients for use in your own brave baking endeavors. Simple browsing sends you right to intriguing varieties of Petal Dust, Edible Pearls and Gumpaste Flower Leaves. You'll also notice tools, cake pans, molds and airbrush supplies. If the idea of doing this yourself is still too scary, just use the resources menu to locate a cake decorator in your area.

DIY	FOOD	

718-771-7628   **Cameras101.com**

If a million monkeys on a million typewriters can come up with a masterpiece of literature, giving cameras to your wedding guests is bound to result in some fine photography. This photo-specialty site offers a lovely selection of disposable wedding cameras designed to put your friends to work documenting the big day. A diverse array of colors and prints even make it easy to match your reception's decorative scheme, which turns out to be important, because you're also bound to end up with a lot of pictures of your friends taking pictures.

DOCUMENT		

866-846-2519   **CatanFashions.com**

Here's a site the bride and her mom may enjoy together, as it offers a lovely assortment of bridal gowns and some absolutely spectacular mother-of-the-bride dresses. Your next stop will be the Shoes and Handbags categories, respectively, which also feature elegant selections. Being that the brick-and-mortar store behind this site is "the largest bridal and fashion salon in the country at over 54,000 square feet," there's bound to be more here for you to explore. in fact, follow the Accessories link and you'll find a lot more….

APPAREL JEWELRY	ATTENDANTS KEEPSAKES	BRIDE SHOES & ACCESSORIES

800-332-5283   **CattleKate.com**

Given the subject matter, it's shocking just how many web sites are devoted to the sort of old-fashioned, rustic living of the fabled American West. But, it would seem that cowboys and cowgirls are every bit as web savvy as the rest of us. In this case, it's even more awe-inspiring to browse through some clothes that, though made in the modern day, look straight out of the 19th century (that's two behind, for anyone counting). There's also riding attire, a smattering of decorative gifts and of course plenty of the accessories that can transform a simple country music fan into a true cowpoke.

APPAREL GROOM	ATTENDANTS SHOES & ACCESSORIES	BRIDE

CCWSupply.com   800-850-9171

Stack your tiered wedding cake as high as you dare with the help of this site, which covers the special baking needs of such a project. Cake stands, filling, icing and ornamental flourishes go a long way toward making a style of cake that doesn't come along every day and, in case something goes wrong, you may opt to go with one of the decorative, fake cakes, which will continue to look delicious even after everybody's had their dessert.

DIY	FOOD	

ChelseaPaper.com   888-407-2726

A lot of custom invitation and announcement retailers get the job done, but here's one that does so with aplomb. Head to the Wedding section and find plenty of brand-name invitations, engagement announcements and save-the-date cards. The great range of options (tending toward "elegant" far more often than "fun") comes complete with online "proof sheets" that allow you to view how the cards will look once you've contributed your own lines of text, which is invaluable.

STATIONERY		

ChinaBridal.com   800-870-7089

From the traditional to the not-so-traditional (check the section called Las Vegas Wedding), this site offers a lovely assortment of Chinese wedding accoutrements. Okay, so the Vegas option essentially has nothing to do with China, but most of this stuff does. Foremost are the fantastic bridal gowns, which include rich embroidery and gorgeous tailoring. Invitations and paper decorations featuring customary and/or lucky characters and symbols fill out the selection, whether you're embracing or deviating from your own family's traditions.

APPAREL FAVORS & DECOR	ATTENDANTS SHOES & ACCESSORIES	BRIDE

ClassyBride.com
866-925-2779

Without a hint of irony, this site offers rhinestone and embroidered personalization of products like robes, slippers, tank tops, bikinis, boxers and thong panties. A fun way to celebrate a bridal party experience, these novelty items may not, strictly speaking, class up the proceedings, but attendants like your ring bearer and flower girl may particularly appreciate the gesture, especially given in conjunction with one of the site's specialty thank-you cards.

APPAREL GROOM	ATTENDANTS KEEPSAKES	BRIDE SHOES & ACCESSORIES

Costco.com
800-774-2678

If you're already a member of Costco, you'll pretty much know what to expect from this online store. What you might not realize is that membership can prove useful when planning a wedding. First off, there are some great deals on engagement rings and the occasional accessory. You'll also find some well-priced floral arrangements. Most important may be the deals you'll find on wine and champagne, typically one of the bigger costs of a thirsty reception.

FLOWERS	JEWELRY	

Cufflinks.com
877-283-3565

Lest you think they merely hold French cuffs together, this site is here to show us all that cufflinks can be. This begins with a bounty of engravable sterling silver and gold designs, some boasting gems and a bevy of thematic shapes owing to such interests as Sports, Music, Transportation, Local Interests (mostly major US cities), Career Related interests and the Military. Most intriguing, however, are the Functional cufflinks found here, which embed such useful items as watches, compasses and thermometers. We suggest consulting with the bride before getting anything too interesting, though.

GROOM	JEWELRY	

Custom-Programs.com   877-300-5290

As it sounds, this useful but very complicated site offers custom programs for your wedding day. Start planning your ceremony's schedule far enough in advance and you may order viewing samples of your foldover, booklet or fan-style programs. In fact, you'll want to give yourself at least thirty days to get your order finalized, proofed and printed, and at least one day more than that to figure out the site's navigation.

DOCUMENT	STATIONERY	

CyberIslandShops.com   888-974-3557

Everybody's got a different idea of what constitutes paradise. For some, it's marriage, for others it involves an island. Here's a site that caters to the cross-section of these folk, offering a bevy of beachy favors and accessories. Sand dollars, cockleshells, starfish and sea glass comprise several sections of reception accents to match such things as sand castle centerpieces and lighthouse place settings. Or, if you think paradise exists only in fairy tales, this site can guide you to plenty of appropriately fantastic decor as well.

FAVORS & DECOR		

DaisyArts.com   310-396-8463

Boasting a "unique quality and aesthetic that comes from hundreds of years of tradition," this intriguing album and journal producer offers leather, hand-bound books as made by Italian craftsmen. Impeccable gifts and stylish accessories to the creative, organized or nostalgic, the selection of photo albums, picture frames, sketchbooks and journals here exceed all others in terms of quality, if not quantity, and it's hard to imagine guest books or wedding albums looking better.

DOCUMENT	KEEPSAKES	

888-470-4950   DavenportHouse.com

Select the Weddings section of this "English Country Store" (if that's not too obvious) and you'll be greeted with the option of browsing through categories like Elegant Receptions, Guest Favors, Ceremony and Gifts for various members of the wedding party. Inside, the items prove to be, well, English and elegant, which is to say pleasing to genteel folk. From Stunning Centerpieces to Lasting Memories, these items won't make for a party that rocks, but it'll sure make the photos come out looking real nice.

ATTENDANTS KEEPSAKES	DOCUMENT STATIONERY	FAVORS & DECOR

877-923-2743   DavidsBridalGifts.com

This rather large boutique is prepared to overwhelm you with personalized attendants gifts, keepsakes, ceremony accessories and reception bric-a-brac. It's nothing you haven't seen or imagined before, but as it's all tied together by an extensive Wedding Library, which includes books on etiquette and plenty of wedding planning guides, the shop proves itself a valuable resource. Indeed, David and company seem to have thought of everything, right down to some luggage sets to take on the honeymoon; which means less thinking for you.

FAVORS & DECOR	KEEPSAKES	

011 39 864 253070   DiCarlo.it

Begin browsing this Italian site by finding the English Version link midway down the right side of the home page. Once in, you'll find a beautiful and tasty bevy of Italian treats for use as edible wedding favors. Foremost is the Confetti, which is sort of like the paper confetti we typically think of, except it's made with chocolate, nuts and a lustrous candy coating. If you think these are nice, wait until you see the Flowers of Sulmona. You guessed it—they're not flowers at all, but favors made to look like flowers, crafted by the aforementioned confetti. Buono!

FAVORS & DECOR	FOOD	

DiscountDesignerMensWear.com 866-761-1500

The word *menswear* sounds generic and dull, which doesn't in any way apply to the fine designer duds offered by this site. *Discounts*, on the other hand, gets the adrenaline pumping, and a bargain is exactly what you can expect to find here. From short to big sizes, and plenty between, browsing these rudimentarily built pages will turn up a bevy of great, reasonably priced dress suits and formalwear, featuring brand names such as Ralph Lauren, Oleg Cassini and Nino Cardi suits and tuxedoes. Tons of cachet, not so much cost.

APPAREL	ATTENDANTS	GROOM

DivineDelights.com 800-443-2836

Redefining what it means to be a cake, this Northern California bakery offers exquisitely packaged and decorated petit fours, as well as a deceptively simple combination of flavors. Incorporating fruits and spices into their sweet concoctions, these guys promise a "taste of heaven," and if the pictures are any indication, they deliver. The only problem you may encounter is that these petit fours are so reasonably priced and delicious looking that it might be hard to stop yourself from eating two, four, eight or an entire thirty-six-cake package before the guests even arrive.

FOOD		

DressesOnline.com 805-520-3656

A slew of beautiful dresses awaits your bridesmaids in this special-occasion dress shop. With formal gowns, evening gowns and prom dresses, all they seem to be missing are wedding gowns. However, the Bridesmaid and Plus Sizes categories are the ones to focus on here, offering elegant and sexy dresses in a variety of styles and colors. Any close girlfriend would jump at the chance to wear these gowns, especially given how reasonable the prices turn out to be.

APPAREL	ATTENDANTS	

888-393-2253   DyeableShoeStore.com

Let's face it; if you let any one of your bridesmaids wear too nice a dress, you run the risk that she'll outshine the bride. In other words, you're going to put your best girlfriends in frocks better suited to the pages of a comic book than a fashion magazine. However, allow each of them a nice pair of shoes and they might just forgive you. This dyeable shoe specialist can help you find affordable pairs of shoes that the girls may even enjoy wearing on subsequent occasions, meaning everybody can stay friends.

ATTENDANTS	SHOES & ACCESSORIES	

812-944-3283   EarthlyGoods.com

Garden lovers will enjoy this site, which offers very special invitations and announcements that will get your message to friends and family, and beautify the planet in the process. Personalized and design-your-own seed packets allow you to spruce up the traditional invite, and then may be planted to grow into your choice of wildflowers, herbs and even vegetables. The fun doesn't stop there, as personalized, recycled flowerpots make terrific favors for your earth-friendly reception. Minimum orders may apply, but in some cases assembling the products yourself will land you a sweet deal.

DIY	FAVORS & DECOR	STATIONERY

212-239-6505   eDressMe.com

Dresses for special occasions and other nights out comprise the bulk of this site's catalog. Split into categories like Evening Dresses, Cocktail Dresses, Little Black Dresses, Plus Size and Tango Dresses, the selection includes fashion labels like BCBG and Nicole Miller, as well as some trendy, relatively anonymous alternatives. While the very cluttered menu may seem daunting at first, if you look close you'll see it can lead you quickly to terrific sale items, as well as specialty gowns for weddings.

APPAREL	ATTENDANTS	

eInvite.com   888-346-8483

Making your invitation shopping a simple matter is this online stationer with a
name so obvious it might easily be overlooked. However, with wedding invitation
categories like Traditional, Modern, Latest Trends, Lavish Looks and Affordable
Choices, the slickly made site really does do a lot to make your experience smooth
as can be. A few clicks will lead you straight to what you need, whether it's bridal
shower invitations or programs, and personalization software allows you to put
together samples right on your screen. Don't miss it.

STATIONERY		

Elegant-Party-Favors.com   818-980-5368

This wedding favor specialist offers only a slim assortment of wares, pretty much
restricted to napkins, matchbooks, memo pads and candy. As it turns out, were
there more to choose from, ordering would be too much of a headache. It's already
a pain, and we wouldn't even mention it except for the lovely personalization
options. As difficult as it may be to manually sort out colors and typesets, fill in
the order form with the appropriate product code numbers, the results speak for
themselves, and we reluctantly approve.

FAVORS & DECOR		

ElegantCheesecakes.com   650-728-2248

When money is no object and exquisite presentation is as important as decadent
taste, take a look at these extraordinary cheesecake wedding favors. Artistically
rendered as small presents with floral bows, these sumptuous treats are available
in dozens of mouth-watering flavors such as vanilla bourbon, white chocolate
pistachio and chocolate coffee hazelnut praline. At roughly twenty-five dollars
per cake (more if you personalize), these are not for everybody, but if you look
at the chef's wedding cake gallery, you might want to phone in a special order so
everybody can try a piece.

FAVORS & DECOR	FOOD	

212-255-7990 — Elenis.com

Brownies, Candies, Cookies and Cupcakes. That's what you'll find in the Sweet Shop section of this site, and what else would you need to know? How about the fact these sweets are "made with the finest all-natural ingredients?" Or that the cupcakes offer "hand-iced shapes and whimsical designs?" Any way you look at it, if you view the site you're bound to come away with some sweet, delicious favors from this "homespun" bakery out of New York's Chelsea neighborhood.

FAVORS & DECOR	FOOD	

800-652-5002 — Emitations.com

Boasting "affordable elegance," this faux-jewelry shop offers designer-, vintage-, trend- and celebrity-inspired baubles for any occasion, the list of which happens to include weddings. Brooches, tiaras, hair combs and endless styles of bridal jewelry range in price from affordable to cheap. These copied designs may not last as long as the real thing, but since you only get married once (we hope), you'll never need to wear them again. With the money you save, you can upgrade that honeymoon.

ATTENDANTS	BRIDE	JEWELRY

866-372-2731 — EscapeConcepts.com

This is the kind of site where the proprietors put so much time, energy and resources into gathering a wonderful, deep selection that they had little left to put toward user-friendliness. The result is one of the more interesting assortments of wedding favors out there, scattered across several different categories that are at times too distinct and otherwise overlapping. Nevertheless, the personalized gifts and bric-a-brac for your attendants and guests are worth a look; a long one if you have the patience.

ATTENDANTS KEEPSAKES	FAVORS & DECOR PARTIES	FOOD STATIONERY

eWeddingAccessories.com · 800-230-3913

Beginning with tiaras and hairpins, and ending with shoes, here's a site that attends to the bride's accessorizing needs. You'll find some exquisite pearl and jeweled pieces, including earrings, necklaces and bracelets, that provide multiple matching options. Same goes with the bridal shoes and handbags, which incorporate lovely materials with classic designs. You may also want to match ceremony accessories, like ring pillows and flower baskets, which are on par with the elegance of some toasting flutes and guest books. Rarely do you find such elegant items on a site starting with a small *e*.

BRIDE SHOES & ACCESSORIES	FAVORS & DECOR	JEWELRY

eWeddingShoes.com · 877-823-1500

Not surprisingly, this somewhat girly-looking site is set up to serve the interests of, well, girls. Rather, it's meant to accommodate the dreams of any girl who's grown up into a ravishing bride-to-be, a woman of some taste who demands that her wedding should be exactly as she has always envisioned: with her at the sparkling center. To this end, it's got shoes by Entrata and Vera Wang, along with gorgeous handbags, hairpins and bridal jewelry, and absolutely nothing for the groom to see before the big day.

ATTENDANTS SHOES & ACCESSORIES	BRIDE	JEWELRY

ExclusivelyWeddings.com · 800-759-7666

Who will prefer to shop for wedding favors and accessories here rather than elsewhere? Well, if the site is to be believed, only "discriminating brides." The rest of you can stick to hand-whittled cake tops and crayon-drawn invitations, apparently. This place offers an elegant, if inexpensive, assortment of things like garters, wedding party gifts and invitations. Pretty much it encompasses all of the little material details that need to be procured between the proposal and the "I Do," and even some "reception sneakers," for discriminating postnuptial joggers. Talk about thorough.

ATTENDANTS KEEPSAKES	FAVORS & DECOR SHOES & ACCESSORIES	JEWELRY STATIONERY

800-521-5443   **FabulousStationery.com**

If you take note and thank-you cards seriously, you'll want to shop from this ad agency that has made its in-house stationery designs available to a public market. And there are plenty to choose from, all with bright colors and distinctive modern designs. As if the tremendous variety weren't enough, they offer to personalize these sets with your name and address, which are incorporated into the cards' visual style, ensuring that your thank -you card set is perfect inside and out.

STATIONERY		

818-981-3727   **FaireFrouFrou.com**

In French, the name of this lingerie boutique means "to show off," and there's an abundance of gorgeous and exquisitely sexy attire here for the bride who wishes to flaunt it on her wedding night. Don't make the mistake of thinking these garments are over-the-top, though, as there's usually an underlying sweetness and elegance that beautifully backs up this boutique's claim to be a "celebration of all that is feminine and flirty."

APPAREL	BRIDE	

406-522-8887   **FancyFlours.com**

This wedding cake specialty shop offers "a fabulous selection of difficult-to-find ingredients and delightful edible sugar whimsies to make even the simplest creation special." Starting quite literally at the top is a charming selection of vintage cake toppers, including several ethnic and French varieties and dating as far back as the 1920s. There are also cake pans, recipes and ingredients aplenty, giving you the freedom to make a wedding cake unlike any other.

DIY KEEPSAKES	FAVORS & DECOR	FOOD

• wedding shops •

FavorAffair.com 866-586-5293

With enough favors that you could place a different one at every table setting, this specialty shop offers just about everything imaginable, from edible favors to candles, soaps, silver keepsakes and shells. Because its selection is so focused, you may browse specific categories like Cookies and Beach Weddings; each filled with so many choices it could almost warrant its own specialty shop. This one could hold your attention for a while.

ATTENDANTS	FAVORS & DECOR	KEEPSAKES

Favors4Weddings.com 888-315-7333

Another lovely and environmentally friendly favor choice is made available from this site. It offers plantable seed packets that will grow into lavender, calla lilies, herb gardens, wildflowers and more. Finding all of the different options can be difficult on this site that often seems as scattered as windblown dandelion seeds, but if you stick to it, you're pretty much guaranteed that something beautiful will grow out of your wedding day.

FAVORS & DECOR	FLOWERS	

FavorsByLisa.com 203-336-0011

This all-around great site offers a variety of thematic invitation and decoration options, many of which may offer a little inspiration if not perfection. You'll find a small assortment of wedding favors, including petal cones for a lovely wedding toss and gorgeous components for elegant place settings. In most cases the prices are outrageously low for what you're getting, which creates a nice atmosphere of all-around savings. If you're planning on a dream wedding and want to keep overhead down, you'll definitely want to check this one out at least once.

FAVORS & DECOR	FOOD	PARTIES

877-597-0234 **FavorsEtc.com**

If you'd like your names to be as memorable as the occasion, get personal with this site, which turns out to be much better than it looks. Personalized and do-it-yourself favors, favor packaging, tablewares and keepsakes abound, offering you every opportunity to etch, engrave, emboss or print your names or initials on decorative and functional items such as matchbooks, napkins, toasting flutes, cake servers, guest towels, ribbons and coasters. Of course, you'll have the option to order blank versions of these products, but why would you want to do that?

DIY KEEPSAKES	DOCUMENT STATIONERY	FAVORS & DECOR

800-320-2664 **FByS.com**

Checking off the minutia of both a ceremony and reception can be taxing, and you may start wondering what you got yourself into. This site can take some of the load off your mind, offering plenty of the small items that you don't want to do without, but don't want to think about either. An incredible abundance of unique and personalized favors complements the toasting flutes, cake servers, wedding tosses and place-card holders that make up the better part of this selection, rounded out by some of the sweetest flower girl accessories online. Shop here, and free your mind to worry about things like where to seat your future in-laws.

FAVORS & DECOR SHOES & ACCESSORIES	FOOD	KEEPSAKES

925-299-6761 **Festivale.net**

Beginning with invitations, this site offers a rather personal touch, specializing in handmade wedding items. You'll also find some gorgeous favors and favor boxes, alongside a small variety of thematic decorations and the quaintest assortment of ring pillows anywhere. Of course, it is the invitations that stand out the most, incorporating hand-crafted paper and personalized calligraphy with adorable contemporary and traditional designs. Always worth a look.

FAVORS & DECOR STATIONERY	JEWELRY	SHOES & ACCESSORIES

FiligreeMonograms.com   707-537-0574

As you might have guessed, this unique site's specialty is monogramming. What's less easy to figure out is what exactly it's willing to monogram. The often perplexing site may seem a little unfocused, but if you look closely you'll see it offers such interesting items as personalized table runners, toasting flute ribbons and handbags. The handbags make for lovely bridesmaid gifts, while the ribbons and runners may be cherished as keepsakes, even if you never imagined such things before.

ATTENDANTS	KEEPSAKES	SHOES & ACCESSORIES

FineStationery.com   888-808-3463

Don't let the word *fine* deter the fun-loving stationery customer. While the bulk of this site surely qualifies as elegant, sophisticated and/or refined, there's just enough whimsy here to keep the shop from having the atmosphere of a mausoleum. Similarly, there's no reason to fear exorbitant pricing, especially if you steer clear of those selections marked by the $$$ symbol (look familiar?). What you can look forward to is a thorough selection including thank-you card sets, invitations for myriad wedding styles and themes. In other words, just fine.

STATIONERY		

FlaskShop.com   800-962-5003

It's probably not necessary to encourage your groomsmen to drink, but a nice flask sure makes an appreciative thank-you gift. Better yet, fill the flasks with a fine scotch before you give it to them, and even the photo sessions will be a good time. This specialty shop offers a terrific selection, many of which may be personalized with laser engraving, or even with a custom photo. Of course, if you're in a hurry you can just go for the ones decorated with pinup girls.

GROOM		

877-522-1630   **FlowersForRent.com**

Promising "fairy-tale flowers for a real budget," the affordability of this floral wedding specialist is twofold: first, these are artificial flowers, available regardless of season and able to withstand any weather conditions. Second, they are not for purchase, but for rent. Reserve your bouquets and centerpieces well in advance to receive them up to three weeks before your wedding date and you'll have three weeks after to return them using the provided postage-paid envelope.

FLOWERS		

800-424-8973   **Fonts.com**

Printing your own invitations and programs is not very difficult to do, and can save you a lot of money. Of course, you'll want a script as elegant looking as any professional stationer would provide, which is why this site proves indispensable. Take a look at the Calligraphic Fonts section of this font software store and view hundreds of different calligraphy styles, each easily and affordably downloaded for use in your do-it-yourself stationery endeavors.

DIY	STATIONERY	

800-367-8866   **Fortunoff.com**

From modest beginnings as a neighborhood housewares store in Brooklyn, Fortunoff shops have expanded over nearly eight decades to finally bring their great selection and prices online. This includes a tremendous bridal registry, of course, but also some incredibly fine bridal jewelry, wedding bands and engagement rings, as well as some upscale attendant gifts. These gifts may not satisfy your bridesmaids and groomsmen quite as much as one of these diamond rings will please the bride, but they should come pretty close.

ATTENDANTS	JEWELRY	SHOES & ACCESSORIES

ForYourParty.com   866-383-8957

Throwing a party can be as simple as calling some friends and putting a bowl of
peanuts on your coffee table. But when you really want to go all out, this is the
site to visit. Personalized napkins, coasters, matchbooks and favors will turn your
fete into a festive event whether it's a wedding, bridal shower, rehearsal dinner
or a surprisingly well-organized bachelor party. For the latter you'll still want to
include the peanuts.

FAVORS & DECOR	STATIONERY	

Fredericks.com   602-760-2111

Behind the tagline "be a white hot bride," this lingerie mainstay makes it quite
easy for the new Mrs. to outfit a month's worth of honeymooning. Garters, hosiery
and shapewear will give the bride a sexy turn on her big day, and a huge catalog of
every underthing worth mentioning will keep you busy browsing, but it's without
a doubt the bridal section of this site that will attract the most attention, with
beautiful white corsets, bras and items best left unmentionable.

APPAREL	BRIDE	

FreshRoses.com   800-880-0735

Whether you want to arrange your own bouquet, reception centerpieces or
both, here's a nice little web shop for the do-it-yourselfer. Despite the site's
name, there is plenty more than roses here, with a long list of flowers available
seasonally, including tulips, lilies, gardenias, garlands, hydrangeas, snapdragons
and daffodils. The best part is that every single one comes straight from the
grower, making them as fresh as they are affordable.

DIY	FLOWERS	

323-655-2988 GaraDanielle.com

To get to this site's unique selection, follow the Jewelry link from the home page, then find "click here to visit our online store." This will be your path to a great assortment of handmade cameos, pendants and earrings. Now, the term *handmade* is tossed around a lot, so we'd like to emphasize the fact that these products are often actually hand-carved from precious stones, frequently incorporating flower and animal shapes. You won't find anything like this elsewhere, and there's enough here that, if you wade through the overcomplicated links and pages, you're sure to find something pretty amazing.

ATTENDANTS	BRIDE	JEWELRY

800-244-5232 GiftsIn24.com

To personalize the paper products for your wedding, beginning with place cards and going on to include coasters and napkins, check out this retailer with a background in gifts. There aren't a huge number of options on the site these days, but given that you can print or emboss those products that are available, they may be worth more than they initially seem. The result is an elegant statement that you planned ahead for every detail of this wedding.

FAVORS & DECOR		

800-725-7664 GiftSongs.com

This site offers an unusual and not in the slightest bit cheesy service: a personalized song for your wedding. By personalized, we mean you can type in the bride and groom's names and one of the site's dozens of original songs will be altered and recorded to specifically praise their love. This could turn out to be very sweet, or very silly, but it will certainly be unforgettable.

FAVORS & DECOR	KEEPSAKES	

GiveMyRegardsTo.com   612-929-3373

Neither the best-stocked nor easiest-to-use stationer online, this shop's charms lie not in its overwhelming supply of invitations so much as in its save-the-date cards and personalized stationery. The cards are very cute; good for bridal showers and bachelorette parties as well for informal weddings. The stationery sets prove equally fun, and should make lovely bridesmaid, flower girl and ring bearer gifts.

ATTENDANTS | **STATIONERY**

Godiva.com   800-946-3482

For wedding favors that are truly worthy of indulgence, check out the offerings of this world-renowned chocolatier, which has long been in the business of pleasing taste buds with smooth, flavorful chocolate and rich, creamy middles. A special Wedding & Party Favors section makes it incredibly easy to stock up on the decadent confections, which are often heart-shaped and always beautifully packaged. Your guests will thank you.

FOOD

GoodFortunes.com   800-644-9474

Everybody likes cookies, and this holds especially true when they spread messages of prosperity and joy. That's what you can expect from this fortune cookie specialist that offers a surprisingly diverse assortment of edible wedding favors. Aside from iced and decorated fortune cookies in several sizes, you'll find dipped Oreos and an abundance of cookies that can be personalized with an embedded photograph. If you liked cookies before you'll positively love them once you've seen this site.

FAVORS & DECOR | **FOOD**

877-760-5259 # Grammies-Attic.com

Special occasions call for special attire, and for your infant or toddler you may not find lovelier garments than those offered by this odd-looking but surprisingly functional site. New, vintage and retro-inspired christening gowns, layette and pinafores will make your favorite adorable tot one of the best-dressed guests at your wedding.

APPAREL	ATTENDANTS	

800-825-5122 # GreenWorldProject.net

Wouldn't this world be more wonderful if everyone who attended your wedding planted a tree? With spruce seedlings packaged into save-the-date cards or special wedding favors, your nuptials will almost certainly result in the successful planting of several new trees. You may even buy bulk orders of the seedlings to be used in invitations and favors of your own devise. It sounds hopelessly idealistic, but this site might just thwart the cynic in us all.

DIY	FAVORS & DECOR	STATIONERY

866-694-7666 # GroomsOnlineGifts.com

There are myriad sites out there catering to brides and grooms wishing to bestow attendant gifts on their entire bridal party. But let's face it; most bridal boutiques aren't exactly designed with the masculine interest in mind. This groomsman gift specialty shop delves deeper into the world of men's gifts, offering thoughtful, personalized products for the guy's guy, whether he's a carefree bachelor, a little gray about the edges or a wee little ring bearer. More rugged than your typical gift shop, this is the rare wedding site that will be appreciated by those fellas willing to wear a tuxedo for you.

ATTENDANTS	GROOM	

GroomStand.com

866-500-2036

If this site is any indication, procuring gifts to thank your groomsmen will be some of the most fun shopping you do leading up to the big day. The usual suspects are available, such as cufflinks, pocketknives and flasks, and like most of the products here may be engraved. But you'll also find gadgets, golf accessories, money clips and executive toys, as well as a smattering of items to give your other attendants, young and old. Heck, you might even find something for yourself.

GROOM

GroomStop.com

469-222-4510

They're renting tuxes, seating your guests and standing by you in your most nerve-wrecked hour, and all your groomsmen and ushers expect in return is a token gift, and maybe a wild bachelor party. The party part is up to them, but the gifts fall into your hands— don't worry; they just happen to be this site's specialty. Its charm doesn't lie in originality; this catalog includes all the same things found elsewhere: flasks, pocketknives, cigar accessories, golf toys and barware. The difference is that here you'll find a much bigger selection of each of these items than anywhere else, and that's enough to make even the stripper happy.

GROOM

HairComesTheBride.com

800-485-4444

Complete with hair and makeup tips, this terrific specialty site is here to help the bride look her absolute best. Follow the link to the Boutique and you'll find one of the web's best assortments of tiaras, hairpins, combs, veils and every other imaginable headpiece, including extensions. Look further and you'll see some elegant bridal jewelry, a lovely smattering of shoes and plenty of pretty purses. You might even find an adorable dress for the second prettiest person at the party: the flower girl.

ATTENDANTS SHOES & ACCESSORIES | BRIDE | JEWELRY

HandBagArt.com

We don't come by handbags like this very often, and we look at a lot of handbags. These special designs incorporate fur, python skin and/or Swarovski crystals, resulting in glamorous evening bags that will look great with a wedding dress, or be a much appreciated attendants gift. The thing is, there are only a few options available, so you'll want to look at them all before deciding just how special you want your purses to be.

ATTENDANTS	BRIDE	SHOES & ACCESSORIES

800-840-3660
HawaiianTropicals.com

There are certain types of flowers that people expect to see at a wedding: roses, tulips, daisies, sunflowers, violets and the dreaded carnations. This site offers a surefire way to surprise and delight your guests, with arrangements featuring beautiful tropical flowers from the Aloha State. Orchids and birds of paradise are just some of the exotic flowers that turn up in arrangements that will work as bouquets, leis and centerpieces, and in every case the colors are magnificent.

FAVORS & DECOR	FLOWERS	

808-833-9900
HawaiianWeddingShop.com

Say *Mahalo* to this Hawaiian wedding specialist and its lovely assortment of simple and beautiful bridal gowns. Whether you're planning a beach theme reception, an island destination wedding or just love the spirit of Aloha, this site is sure to please, stocked with unique and memorable favors, attendant gifts, hair accessories, gorgeous centerpieces and, of course, leis. It makes you wonder why anybody ever gets married indoors.

APPAREL FLOWERS	BRIDE JEWELRY	FAVORS & DECOR SHOES & ACCESSORIES

HerRoom.com   800-558-677•

This lingerie site promises the sort of day-to-day underwear a woman will likel•
buy for herself, but that isn't to say you won't find a little something sexy for th•
honeymoon. A Bridal section guides you quickly to products meant to accentuat•
your sex appeal, beginning with a wide range of garter belts and bustiers, but th•
bulk of the site will help you find important necessities like strapless bras an•
shapewear to ensure your dress looks spectacular.

| APPAREL | BRIDE | |

HipsAndCurves.com   800-220-887•

Welcome to the web site where fuller figures take an erotic turn. Offering sexy far•
constructed of lace, mesh, vinyl and patent leather, these intimates accommodat•
a variety of sensuous tastes, whether they include costuming, garter belts, bod•
stockings or more romantic inclinations. Tasteful yet exotic displays make thi•
one of the steamier sites online, which bodes well for your honeymoon.

| APPAREL | BRIDE | |

HouseOfBrides.com   800-395-124•

When you're ready to spend several days browsing bridal and bridesmaid attire•
check out this, the "World's Largest Online Wedding Store." While we can't bac•
any claim that it's the biggest, we can vouch for its humongous selection, coverin•
every wedding-related dress you'll need, including maternity and plus sizes, a•
well as dresses for the flower girl and mother of the bride. While the page desig•
is typical among all e-commerce sites, with the incredible size of this shop, usin•
it proves uncharacteristically difficult—you really might be here for days!

| APPAREL | ATTENDANTS | BRIDE |
| DOCUMENT | KEEPSAKES | SHOES & ACCESSORIES |

877-388-8088 **iBlossom.com**

When it comes to artificial flowers, only one material is really going to do any justice to the real thing: silk. So, while actual rose petals sprinkled in the aisle or used as a wedding toss might be very special, silk rose petals might be seen as just that much more special (plus, they won't stain the ground the way real roses do). While you're perusing this shop's many available petal colors, take a quick peek at the beautiful silk bouquets; not only are they lovely, but they'll never die on you.

FLOWERS

800-621-2998 **Illuminations.com**

With the power to light up anybody's life, it's hard to beat candles when you want to set a romantic tone, and this site can lead you to some of the most beautiful, sweetest smelling candles available online. With floating candles, scented candles, unscented candles, tealights and a few aromatherapeutic varieties, you'll be up to your earwax in options. Your wedding day will be brighter for having visited this fine retailer.

FAVORS & DECOR

800-804-1960 **ImpressInPrint.com**

It'll be hard to get people to the party if you don't send them a good invitation. At least so goes the reasoning behind this site, which offers a tremendous number of invitations, each pertaining to very specific events. How many Clambake invites can there be? Not as many as there are for Lingerie Showers. Browsing can take a while, but animated menus and fairly thorough organization should help you get through the hundreds of available designs without too much trouble, because it's hard to send a good invitation if you can't find one.

STATIONERY

InFashionKids.com   908-371-1733

This New Jersey–based retailer offers what could only be considered dapper dress clothes for boys, darling dresses for girls and adorable attire for tots. Category headings such as Girls Dresses and Boys Tuxedos make it easy to find wedding-appropriate attire, but even if you opt for a more casual affair, this site will serve you right.

| APPAREL | ATTENDANTS | |

Invitation-Supplies.com   630-769-0230

Engaged couples on a budget will appreciate this site, which offers "wedding invitations for less than $1 each." How do they keep the costs so low? It's simple: they let you do all the work. Basically, you'll start by selecting a background card by color or pattern, including handmade petal paper and cards embedded with silk. You then have the option of adding overlays, embellishments, flowers or charms, as well as selecting envelopes and reply cards. Yes, if you want a great bargain you'll have to piece together and address them by hand, but that could be just the thing to keep idle hands busy until the honeymoon.

| DIY | STATIONERY | |

InvitationBox.com   866-814-4269

Adjust your monitor's brightness and contrast settings before viewing this online stationer, as its extraordinarily pastel veneer can make it difficult to spot the gems of the wide selection of invitations and announcements populating these pages, and you'll need every advantage as you try. Though very well organized, browsing proves a frustrating yet ultimately rewarding process right up until you enter up to a dozen lines of personalized text into the perfect paper product for your event.

| STATIONERY | | |

626-792-5857   InvitationKitchen.com

We already know that do-it-yourself invitations and favor packaging can save you some money, but with this site we also learn that doing so can be a lot of fun. At least, these DIY kits promise fun results, with colorful, lively invites, table place cards, save the dates, enclosures and thank-you card sets. Setting up your personalized stationery can get a little complicated, but once you've gotten through the process you may view PDF files of your work as proofs against errors, ultimately streamlining a process that will net you cool, affordable cards to assemble and mail.

DIY	STATIONERY	

800-257-9567   InvitationsByDawn.com

Finding the right invitations can be a long, arduous process (if you're particular about it), or a breeze (if you're not). This site will make the decision easier for the finicky bride and groom, with invites parsed out by color, wedding theme and style, so you may quickly link to the type of stationery you have in mind. Ironically, this same process is bound to make things harder on easygoing couples, as the terrific variety on display might just start you second-guessing yourselves.

FAVORS & DECOR	STATIONERY	

925-820-6488   Iomoi.com

This unique stationer (and e-stationer) offers plenty when it comes to ingenuity. Unfortunately, it doesn't offer very many of its slickly designed, modern invitations. However, it makes up for any shortcomings by offering a tremendous assortment of very original, personalized labels, as well as stationery gifts for flower girls and bridesmaids. Finally, we can't resist the supercool matchboxes, which will be perfect when it comes time to light the sparklers.

ATTENDANTS	FAVORS & DECOR	STATIONERY

JaneTran.com   213-624-0759

There's little doubt you'll be worried about your hair right up until the moment you walk up the aisle (and possibly for a few moments after that). However, you can always ease your concern by choosing from this designer's gorgeous assortment of bridal hair accessories. Her "love of color and texture and the beauty of form and function" is evident in her crystal, gemstone, shell, coral and pearl creations, and just about every one will look fantastic on your undeniably perfect coif.

BRIDE	SHOES & ACCESSORIES	

JCrew.com   800-562-0258

Just when we thought we had the J. Crew catalog figured out, we discovered the web site's Wedding and Party Store, a full section of the shop devoted to brides, grooms, bridesmaids, groomsmen, flower girls and ring bearers. These few simple gowns, dresses, suits and tuxedos can go a long way in providing affordable, not-so-stuffy attire; sort of like the rest of the popular catalog, only with more elegance than a rugby shirt.

APPAREL GROOM	ATTENDANTS	BRIDE

JenniBick.com   800-640-8758

A tremendous source of handmade wedding albums, wedding guest books and journals, this Massachusetts bookbinding company makes and sells fantastic products worthy of preserving the most prestigious moments, outstanding ideas and fondest memories. There may be little difference between categories like Brag Books, Keepsake Books, Scrapbooks and Photo Albums other than style, but browsing through them all will easily be worth the time of anyone who appreciates fine craftsmanship and elegant design.

DOCUMENT	STATIONERY	

800-711-8718   JessicaMcClintock.com

Perhaps you're already familiar with the romantic designs of fashion mainstay Jessica McClintock. However, if you are not, by all means relish this opportunity to get acquainted. Either way, on this site you'll discover a dazzling arsenal of dresses for the bride, bridesmaid and flower girl. Contemporary without being flashy, modern without being nontraditional, these beautiful garments cost much less than you'd imagine, and will make every member of the bridal party ecstatic to be a part of it.

APPAREL SHOES & ACCESSORIES	ATTENDANTS	BRIDE

866-568-6676   JoannSmyth.com

For some lovely, high-end bridal jewelry, check out this Los Angeles jewelry designer's beautiful pearl designs. Follow the Online Catalog link, then select Bridal on the lefthand menu and begin browsing the Bridal subcategories. You'll find a small supply of gorgeous earrings and necklaces that are pricey enough you'll want to insure them along with your engagement ring. Unfortunately, you cannot view these baubles in great detail, but considering Ms. Smyth's clientele includes celebrities such as Nicole Kidman, Jennifer Anniston and Madonna, they're certain to be as lovely as they look.

BRIDE	JEWELRY	

800-510-7149   JoinUsInvitations.com

For luxurious looks in your invitations, visit this small high-end stationer working out of "Chicago's emerging bridal district." Often incorporating the "vintage glamour of a bygone era combined with today's necessary bling," these quality invites and enclosures aren't plenty in number, but the savvy shopper will surely be able to match the elegant designs with available place cards, programs, favors packaging and thank-you cards, making for a beautifully consistent paper trail to your wedding.

FAVORS & DECOR	STATIONERY	

JosephSchmidtConfections.com   866-237-0152

Most of the boxed chocolates offered by this confectioner come with a clear top, and with good reason: these are about the best-looking candies we've ever laid eyes on. There may not be a lot to sort through, but the decorated tops of these truffle, caramel, nut and/or fruit candies are beautiful and distinctive enough that you'll probably spend a good deal of time perusing the site anyway. They almost look too good to eat, and the decadent feeling of biting into one makes it taste all the better.

FAVORS & DECOR	FOOD	

JRCigars.com   888-574-3576

Cigars may not serve any traditional roles in weddings, but bachelor parties have been lighting up ever since before the advent of the stag film. Where better to do your celebratory stogie shopping than a genuine North Carolina tobacconist? From deep in tobacco country, JR Cigars offers a wide selection of both Hand Made and Machine Rolled varieties, covering dozens of discount and high-end brands, including most of the high-quality Central American favorites. Pass them out to your groomsmen, and don't forget to save the best smokes for your new father-in-law.

ATTENDANTS	GROOM	PARTIES

KatesPaperie.com   888-941-9169

Putting a little character into invitations, guest books and wedding albums, this site does so all while providing an enjoyable shopping experience. Styles range from elegant to stuff that'll make your kids giggle, and many of the writing sets, invitations and announcements are available for monogramming. The greatest stuff, however, can be found in the Paper section, which offers different colors, sizes, patterns and materials if you're a do-it-yourselfer.

DIY	DOCUMENT	STATIONERY

310-275-5516   KayaCouture.com

Devoted to children's special-occasion attire, this superb line proves itself special with an incredible selection of girls' dresses. Handmade in the United States, these silk dresses will outfit your flower girl or junior bridesmaid to the envy of every female in attendance, with a smattering of accessories made to match. What this ultimately means is that you better have picked out the greatest wedding gown on the planet, because these garments really raise the bar.

APPAREL	ATTENDANTS	SHOES & ACCESSORIES

800-439-0334   KitBiz.com

If you think all the stuff leading up to the planning of the wedding is complicated, wait until you try to legally change your name! What with your driver's license, social security card, insurance papers, credit cards, bank account, voter registration and passport, the bureaucracy alone is enough to make you consider a common law marriage. This site has assembled kits complete with all the paperwork you'll need to expedite the process. Aside from a bride name change kit, they offer one for both bride and groom, divorce name changes if things turn sour and prenuptial kits if you think things might go sour. It's all about easy.

DOCUMENT		

323-651-1358   LateBloomerStudio.com

We may never know for sure whether flowers make a bride more beautiful, or if it works the other way around. We can tell you, for sure, that this is the web's best source of floral hair clips. These gorgeous silk and bead hair accessories will elegantly frame either formal or casual hairstyles, and are lovely enough to compete with any crystal tiara. However, if you wish to retain the traditional headpiece and veil, you may still wish to consider these pieces to adorn your bridesmaids with something special.

ATTENDANTS SHOES & ACCESSORIES	BRIDE	FLOWERS

LavaHut.com   808-356-097:

The spirit of Aloha is alive and well in e-commerce form on this all-things
Hawaiian lifestyle shop. From grass skirts and dashboard hula girls to silk an
seashell leis, the site has all the classics covered, including the ubiquitous flora
print Hawaiian shirt. However, there are also a lot of great items that may be use
to outfit your island theme wedding, including plenty of serving items and decor
and a lovely assortment of dresses for the bridesmaid. Look hard enough, an
you'll even find a beautiful, affordbale gown for the bride.

APPAREL FAVORS & DECOR	ATTENDANTS	BRIDE

LeeAllison.com   888-434-843

Granted, bow ties aren't the most popular choice in neckwear, but they do seer
to turn up on a lot of grooms. Whether you're looking for something in classi
black silk or wish to opt for something untraditional, this site can outfit yo
with a beautiful, unique and/or conversational tie or bow tie, with silk vests an
cummerbunds to match. The shop can be a lot of fun, but please consult your brid
before purchasing any golf-theme neckwear.

GROOM	SHOES & ACCESSORIES	

LittleGirlDresses.com   866-239-125:

Do little children enjoy dressing up for fancy occasions? Usually not. But tha
doesn't keep us from making them do it. Probably because they look so dar
cute, we subject them to wearing white satin dresses and three-piece suits, the
take them to churches, weddings and other dressy events and show them off wit
style. This site offers a lovely variety of such apparel, and not just for little girls
Communion dresses and suits are backed up by christening gowns, bris gowns an
even ring bearer tuxedos. It's all easy to browse; in fact, the only hard part will b
keeping them clean.

APPAREL	ATTENDANTS	

44-20-7930-8720 — Longmire.co.uk

How much are you wiling to spend on cufflinks? Wait—don't answer that until you've taken a good, long look at this English specialty jeweler's site. Among this astronomically expensive selection you'll find timeless silver looks, high-concept modern designs, startlingly appealing novelty pieces and even a few great-looking monogrammed models. Of course those featuring gemstones are the priciest on the site, but when you're looking at arguably the finest men's jewelry you expect a staggering cost; you just hope it's not going to be in pounds sterling.

GROOM	JEWELRY	

800-980-5893 — LuxePaperie.com

With a lovely selection of boutique stationery brands, this little online paper goods retailer offers a unique assortment of note cards, greeting cards, invitations and wrapping paper. Light colors and simple designs prevent these designs from standing out too much, but the nice-looking cards and paper prove simple to browse, and a Shop By Occasion feature ensures you may quickly find the appropriate messages and illustrations for your wedding, even if the terrific featured brands turn out to be so obscure you've never heard of them.

STATIONERY		

888-332-8610 — MadisonAndFriends.com

This Chicago boutique initially offered designer fashions for babies and toddlers, but like the children it catered to, the shop quickly outgrew its own selection. Now it offers hip apparel and shoes for babies on through preteens, featuring top labels most of us won't be able to find locally, or even elsewhere online. The designer jeans, cool shoes and other upscale kiddie attire are quite hip, but as it turns out, the boutique still knows how to dress a flower girl in the most darling dresses imaginable.

APPAREL	ATTENDANTS	

MagicMomentsCollections.com   631-474-264'

This special-occasion specialist out of Long Island, New York, excels in findin
beautiful dresses for women, teens and young girls. Enter the Bridesmaid, Junic
or Flower Girl categories and you'll see what looks like an adorable little selectio
of gowns. However, these are just the menus of name brands available, includin
the likes of Bari Jay, Jessica McClintock, Mori Lee and Alfred Angelo. Some o
these names might not strike an immediate chord, but in the world of brida
attendants attire, they strike gold.

APPAREL	ATTENDANTS

MarieBelle.com   866-925-880(

There's not normally that much to see when you're looking at chocolate, an
it's not typically around long enough to observe anyway. This selection i
different, though, in an extraordinary way. In some cases here, the confection
have packaging beautiful enough to rival any favor boxes. In other cases, th
chocolates themselves have been turned into canvases for some extraordinary
artistically rendered decorations. These elegant edibles literally look too good t
eat. On the other hand, they look too delicious not to.

FAVORS & DECOR	FOOD

MaternityMall.com   800-466-622:

This maternity megasite has swallowed some of our favorite maternity store
into one huge shop. Consequently, this is where to go when you want to sho
iMaternity, Motherhood or A Pea in the Pod selections. Each caters to subtl
different budgets and styles, but check out the Special Occasion sections of eac
and you'll find lovely formal and semiformal gowns that will work beautifully a
maternity bridesmaid dresses.

APPAREL	ATTENDANTS

800-289-3462   MichaelCFina.com

There are gifts, and then there are gifts. This site specializes in the latter, with presents you don't just haphazardly dole out to friends—at least, not unless your bank balance is written in stanzas. The very high-end assortment of merchandise starts with picture frames and ending somewhere in the jewelry section; whether you're picking something up for the bride (think engagement ring) or her attendants, this will make for some very happy women.

ATTENDANTS JEWELRY	BRIDE	GROOM

877-645-2793   MikaWed.com

This site is much better than it looks, offering a generous assortment of bridal attire and accessories. We think it may be worth a look, especially for the bride who likes to take in all of her options before making a decision. Once you click past the home page, a left-side menu directs you to general categories, but you'll want to take advantage of a subcategory pull-down menu located at the top-middle of the page, to avoid boredom while browsing. If all else fails, you may at least appreciate some adorable flower girl dresses.

APPAREL JEWELRY	ATTENDANTS SHOES & ACCESSORIES	BRIDE

888-701-2323   MikiMotoAmerica.com

When a bride wants to look glamorous and sophisticated, she wears pearls. When she wants to look glamorous and sophisticated and feel like a million bucks, she wears the cultured pearls offered by this jewelry specialist. Okay, so these strands, earrings and pendants aren't quite worth a million, but they don't come cheap, so don't tempt yourself with their luminescent beauty unless you're willing to procure some bridal jewelry that will stay in the family for a long time as a prized and valuable heirloom.

BRIDE	JEWELRY	

MisterShop.com   800-715-797

If finding a designer suit at a reasonable price is important to you, this site wil
become important to you. With categories featuring Ralph Lauren, Calvin Klei
and Ben Sherman, the simple but effective navigation can guide you quickly t
a limited number of prestigious ensembles. We wouldn't recommend this sho
if you value huge assortments of suits in every conceivable style and colo
However, given that the groom and his atttendants will probably be wearing black
this proves a great source of fine threads and classy accessories.

APPAREL	GROOM	SHOES & ACCESSORIES

MJTrim.com   800-965-874

If you've found the perfect wedding gown, except that it's missing that specia
something, this site ought to help. Replete with fashionable trim options, rangin
from lace, fur and fringe to braids, rhinestones and ribbons, the materials her
should offer just the right decorative panache to your dress. You'll also fin
buttons, buckles, clasps and other closures, along with a selection of handles, i
case your designer instincts veer toward handbags as well.

APPAREL	DIY	SHOES & ACCESSORIES

ModelBride.com   866-900-045

Founded by a model-turned-cosmetician-and-stylist, this small site offers bride
an abundance of helpful tips on how to do your own hair and makeup. Doing s
will free up your budget for the boutique's small but precious assortment o
bridal accessories, beginning with the recommended makeup and including som
beautiful shoes, jewelry, hair accessories, tiaras and handbags. Comparing th
results to the proprietress is hardly fair, but if you want to see how shopping her
might turn out, take a look at the gallery of happy customers and clients.

BRIDE SHOES & ACCESSORIES	DIY	JEWELRY

212-744-6667   MomsNightOut.com

Dispelling the notion that pregnancy consists primarily of muumuus and bed rest, the Bridal section of this clothing line/boutique lends a touch of glamour to maternity gowns, with a tidy selection of classic designs that have been adjusted ever-so-slightly to accommodate growing bellies. Each frock is well represented with pictures and descriptions, shown complete with accessories (like veils and wraps), which may be either added to your dress order or purchased separately.

APPAREL SHOES & ACCESSORIES	ATTENDANTS	BRIDE

800-666-3372   Mondera.com

Whatever your taste or price range, the odds are good this site will suit your jewelry needs. This should prove particularly handy for betrothed couples looking for the right set of wedding bands, or for grooms-to-be to build a custom engagement ring. Outside of marital items, you may browse by jewelry type or material, which works out fairly well whether you're looking for men's or women's items. Additionally, each category gives you the option of sticking to a particular price range, a fact that men may want to keep from their fiancées.

JEWELRY		

740-366-0604   MonyaCollection.com

Beautiful bridal gowns and bridesmaid dresses are only a click away, thanks to this site. Available in all sizes, these gowns span a wide range of styles, covering rare and beautiful fashion ground, at prices significantly less than outrageous. There may not be as many bridesmaid dresses available, but each of the ten or so classic silhouettes are available in a broad spectrum of colors, meaning this site could be all you need to outfit the women of your bridal party.

APPAREL SHOES & ACCESSORIES	ATTENDANTS	BRIDE

MoonRockPaper.com   800-823-6690

There are likely to be a million memorable moments from your wedding, few of which you'll remember. Fortunately, there are sure to be dozens of objects you'll want to hold on to as reminders. Whatever keepsakes you do decide to preserve, this site offers beautiful, elegant boxes in which to store them. These boxes range in size and shape, and depending on which one you select, you might need to go shop for more potential mementos.

KEEPSAKES		

MooRoo.com   866-666-7661

You may be familiar with the sort of conceptual art that hangs on museum walls, but how about the kind that hangs off your elbow? The handbags and clutches here draw inspiration from unlikely sources, including flamingos, sushi rollers, and rainbow-colored foxes. By the sound of it, you might expect these items to be tacky or kitschy—but, in truth, they're more likely to be seen on the arms of celebrities than pop culture fetishists. Of course, they'd also look terrific on a bride or bridesmaid.

ATTENDANTS	BRIDE	SHOES & ACCESSORIES

MountainCow.com   800-797-6269

Some people like to make their own stationery and invitations in an arts-and-crafts kind of way, using glue, scissors, sparkles, construction paper and whatnot. But for those of us who're computer savvy, this site offers a distinctly less messy way to design our own cards and letterheads. Specifically, you'll find proprietary software that should make it easy for you to create and incorporate good-looking patterns and backgrounds, without any special artistic talent. Different software packages are available, depending on your computer skills and design intentions, but you'll still need to buy your own paper.

DIY	STATIONERY	

212-967-0760   **MoynaBags.com**

"Individually hand-beaded and embroidered by skilled artisans in India," this incredible assortment of handbags is of such fine quality you might have to upgrade your wedding wardrobe to match. Simply put, there is nothing ordinary among these purses, evening bags, bridal handbags and totes, whether they're adorned by glass beads, silver sequins, feathers, semiprecious stones or embroidered suede. You'll find an amazing bag here for any member of the bridal party.

ATTENDANTS	BRIDE	SHOES & ACCESSORIES

866-482-7673   **MR-Roses.com**

Getting your wedding flowers from Ecuador might not immediately seem the best or most efficient idea. However, this grower from South America offers deals on long-stemmed roses and rose petals that are tough to beat. Free shipping from Tuesday through Friday includes bulk orders and multiple colors (Saturday delivery costs a little extra), and you may order up to sixty days in advance to ensure timely arrival, wherein you may lavishly decorate your ceremony on a budget.

DIY	FLOWERS	

800-605-2011   **MyCakeTopper.com**

There are dozens of sites listed in this book that offer sweet, elegant and/or amusing toppers for your wedding cake, and if you look hard enough you may even find some traditional bride-and-groom figurines that bear a passing resemblance to the actual couple. However, on this singular specialty site you don't have to look hard. All you need to do is upload a picture of the prospective Mr. and Mrs., and in roughly a week you will receive your made-to-order cake topper doppelgangers.

FAVORS & DECOR		

MyGatsby.com 888-997-789

With page after page of both traditional and contemporary designs, along wi plenty of personalization options, this "elegant" invitation site can keep y browsing for hours. Follow the Mix 'n Match options offered by the animate lefthand menu to coordinate your own set of envelopments, backing, respon cards and invite embellishments, or simply peruse one of their featured design collections, any of which are available with customized text. If you find the si disorienting, blame it on the preponderance of pastels.

STATIONERY		

MyGlassSlipper.com 866-933-746

This web shop's nod to Cinderella no doubt refers to its elegant selection couture bridal footwear, but there are some more inexpensive options availab to those of us without fairy godmothers, right on down to some comfortable bri flip-flops. However, the site has a lot more to offer, including some hosier shapewear, bridal jewelry and some of the most extravagant cake toppers we'! come across. The bride-to-be can spend quality minutes scouring these page but we're guessing Prince Charming will spend most of his time perusing t comprehensive lingerie section.

APPAREL	ATTENDANTS	BRIDE
FAVORS & DECOR	JEWELRY	SHOES & ACCESSORIES

MyJeanM.com 800-766-859

More than thirty years of experience as a wedding planner gives the Jean behind this site an edge over competitors, especially in the way she "watche current wedding trends closely to provide brides with the best product selection The weddings superstore covers most decorative aspects of your ceremony ar reception, as well as necessary little extras such as favors, attendant gifts ar thank-you cards. As helpful as it is well-stocked, this is one wedding site that always worth a visit.

ATTENDANTS	FAVORS & DECOR	KEEPSAKES
STATIONERY		

866-942-1311   **MyWeddingFavors.com**

Proving once again there is no shortage of wedding favors on the internet, this site offers all of the expected personalized trinkets, boxes and place card holders, and although it looks suspiciously like a half-dozen other sites out there, the truth is this one does it a little better, and it may in fact be the others who are imitators. The number-one benefit to shopping here is a massive selection, but we're just as fond of the great detail offered for each favor; because if you can't see it close up, how can you be sure what is the best?

FAVORS & DECOR		

503-223-5636   **MyWeddingLabels.com**

You can really put a personal stamp on your wedding reception with the help of this specialty site devoted to printing custom labels for a wide variety of uses. Pretty much any kind of fun or functional wedding favor you can think of can be accommodated, whether CDs, water bottles, candy boxes, gift bags or coasters. Of course, you may attach your name and even picture to anything you can tie a tag to, as these made-to-order labels are offered in a wide range of shapes and sizes. Just don't get carried away and pin a tag on your flower girl.

FAVORS & DECOR		

800-289-2843   **NeckTies.com**

Granted, bow ties aren't the most popular choice in neckwear, but all bets are off during a wedding, and when it comes to outfitting the groom and his men, this site will serve you right. Beginning with dozens of color options, you may also find stripes, polka dots and more complex patterns, as well as some really elaborate designs with pictures all over them. Items vary by neck size; freestyle, pre-tied or clip-on designs; and assorted widths like slim line and butterfly. To top it off, they automatically select for you coordinated ascots, cravats, cummerbunds and pocket squares, lest you not feel goofy enough already.

GROOM	SHOES & ACCESSORIES	

NeimanMarcus.com   888-888-475

High-end designer items abound on this site, as in their brick-and-mortar store in particular in their unparalleled selection of fine apparel, gifts and ladies' shoe In fact, the best way to find the department store's terrific Bridal Shop is to follo the Apparel For Her link. here you'll find fantastic shoes, bridesmaid dresses ar some of the best bridal gowns online.

APPAREL	ATTENDANTS	BRIDE

NicoleMaternity.com   888-424-822

With current looks and sleek designs, nearly every product in this catalog offe proof that this is "not your typical maternity wear." Follow the Shop link ar you'll find a lovely assortment of maternity bridal gowns that cinches it. The sli selection alternates between classic and daring gowns, but always manages 1 impress, both in terms of price and style. You'll only need to accessorize with th natural glow of impending motherhood.

APPAREL	ATTENDANTS	BRIDE
SHOES & ACCESSORIES		

Nordstrom.com   888-282-606

You're probably already familiar with this Seattle-based department store, an possibly even its well-rounded web site. What you may not realize is that, if yo look into the Women's section, you'll find a designated Wedding Shop designe to meet the apparel and accessory needs of the bride, mother of the brid bridesmaids and flower girls, including some lovely, affordable wedding dresse jewelry and shoes. As it turns out, the groom and his best men are also covere with suits, shoes and even some smart tuxedos, but they're even less likely 1 realize it.

APPAREL	ATTENDANTS	BRIDE
GROOM	JEWELRY	SHOES & ACCESSORIES

800-521-0584   Now-And-Forever.com

A great many clean and contemporary invitation designs await you on this site—so many, in fact, you'll want to follow the Refine Selection link immediately upon entering the Stationery category. There, you'll be able to narrow down your choices based on your invite budget, primary color/combinations and design themes (which include things like Angels, Hearts, Calla Lilies and the Ocean). Once you've found something you like, it's a relatively simple matter to order samples, or begin entering several extensive pages of personalized text, for what only seems like forever.

STATIONERY		

800-344-8894   OneOfAKindKid.com

Shopping for babies' and children's clothes from this site proves quite satisfying, particularly if you're outfitting them for a wedding. Simply stick to the categories designated Flower Girl Dresses and Ring Bearer Suits and you can't go wrong. Look hard enough and you might even find some appropriate shoes to go with the new outfit. Of course, you may be inspired to pick up a few regular-occasion items if you stick around long enough to browse this impressively comprehensive online boutique.

APPAREL	ATTENDANTS	SHOES & ACCESSORIES

888-538-8224   OurJewishWedding.com

If you're not in the market for a ketubah, this site will be of no use to you. Members of the Jewish faith, on the other hand, will find a beautiful variety of the ornate wedding contracts, numbering in the hundreds. Unfortunately, the site will slow you down, and viewing them all will be impossible. Rather, you should use the pull-down menu filters to localize on them by Artist, Color, Medium (Metal, Giclee, Fabric, etc.), Style, Symbol and/or denominational text. Elsewhere on the site, if you look hard, you'll notice plenty of wedding accessories and other Judaica for the big day. Mazel tov!

DOCUMENT		

PamelasParasols.com   888-333-073

If your ceremony under the sun could use a touch of Southern charm, this sit
is uniquely prepared to outfit your wedding party. You'll find plenty of beautifu
parasols in many colors, with options to include fringe adornments, such a
seashells, feathers, flowers, gemstones or personalized text. If you decide tha
these delightful accoutrements come at too high a price, you may opt for th
simply elegant folding fans instead, lovely alternatives which still fully satisf
the Southern motif. Smelling salts sold separately.

BRIDE	FAVORS & DECOR	SHOES & ACCESSORIES

Paper-Source.com   888-727-371

Maybe the myriad store-bought stationery designs available online felt lacking
or maybe you're an ardent do-it-yourselfer who would rather cancel the part
than send out invitations designed by another. Either way, you'll appreciate th
incredible selection of papers and crafts products available here to help yo
make your own invitations and stationery sets. Imploring you to "Do somethin
creative every day," the site backs up its encouragement with some incredible
high-quality printed pages that almost outdoes the competition even without an
work on your part.

DIY	STATIONERY	

PaperBride.com   800-603-638

Special thank-yous are in order when your girlfriends dress alike to stand by yo
on your wedding day, when your most distant relatives travel half the globe t
bear witness or when the caterer is graceful enough to serve delicious food to you
guests even after you've snapped his or her head off for a trifle. For such occasion
we guide you to this specialty stationer, which understands the stress and strain
that can turn a blushing bride into "Bridezilla," and offers contemporary, tongue
in-cheek thank-you cards to express your gratitude without being saccharine.

STATIONERY		

* wedding shops *

877-777-4660 — PaperMints.com

A bevy of handmade and contemporary wedding invitations are quite easy to view on this cleanly designed site. However, the ordering process might slow you down a bit if you don't pay close attention to what you're doing. While these cards' great looks are clearly visible, if you've got plenty of time to plan, you may opt to order samples first. If you are in a hurry, though, you can cross your fingers and hope that you enter the personalized information into the order form correctly, and just order outright; but take it from this writer, it's always a good idea to have a proofreader handy.

STATIONERY		

800-420-3818 — PaperMojo.com

There's more to the paper world than 8½x11 white pages, and all the proof you'll ever need may be found with this comprehensive web stationer. Pages of many weights, sizes and colors may be found, whether you prefer iridescent stock, flower-infused, embossed, tissue or all-natural paper. Better yet, an incredible array of patterned pages may be found, many evoking the diverse cultural traditions of such countries as Italy, Japan, India and Nepal. You wouldn't use any of this stuff for a resume or school paper, but if you're designing your own invites, they may be perfect.

DIY	STATIONERY	

800-727-3701 — PaperPresentation.com

If you prefer to work with raw materials when it comes to sending invitations, this site ought to be of great help. To begin with, they offer a terrific selection of paper, in multiple weights, colors and textures. Then there are the card stock options, which vary in shape and design, whether you prefer square cards or those that open from the middle, and a selection of envelopes that ranges from the mundane to the sublime. Best of all, many of these products are available on recycled paper, so you can get the word out to everyone you know without suffering any pangs of conscience.

DIY	STATIONERY	

PaperStyle.com

888-670-530

Whether you're planning a formal wedding, or a casual one, you'll be able to fin the appropriate set of invitations on this slow but well-put-together site. Eve if you're looking for some regular stationery, you will find a great big selectio of elegant and/or campy stuff, in most cases easily personalized for no extr cost. But most of these resources are devoted to announcements and invites and it shows (usually with RSVP envelopes included). In fact, browsing might jus inspire you to invite more people.

STATIONERY

PartyLights.com

866-758-583

You can keep the party going all night long with the help of this site, whic specializes in outdoor lighting that sets a festive mood. The shop's outstandin variety of paper lanterns, light strings, upscale lanterns and novelty lamps shoul be enough to accommodate any wedding style or theme, and simply browsing th well-designed pages may even give you some ideas. The honeymoon can alway start at sunup.

FAVORS & DECOR

PastryKisses.com

323-874-4006

Delicious appetizers can get a reception off to a great start and, if you'd like to save money by providing your own, we'd recommend considering this mouthwatering specialty site. There are very few pastry twists available here, but with flavor like Cranberry & Gorgonzola, Cilantro Pesto & Corn, Caramelized Onion & Fet and Blueberry Lemon Cream, they seem to have all your sweet and savory base covered.

FOOD

800-247-8162 — PaulFredrick.com

The Paul Fredrick line of clothes is known to be a quality set of dress attire, but don't make the mistake of thinking they're stuffy. Somehow, these guys have managed to blur the boundaries between casual and chic, with dignified but breezy designs that will have you looking and feeling more comfortable than anybody else in the wedding. Some formalwear, cufflinks and ties are available, but it's always handy to remember that a groom's style can transcend the restrictions imposed by the traditional tuxedo.

APPAREL SHOES & ACCESSORIES	GROOM	JEWELRY

770-455-1800 — PeachTreeCircle.com

If you're looking for wedding charms, this is a great place to start. If you haven't until now thought to look for them, here's what they are: small metal charms in symbolic shapes like that of an engagement ring, baby carriage or shamrock. Per Victorian tradition, these charms are baked into the wedding cake attached to ribbons, which are then tugged by members of the bridal party to portend their futures (in the case of the charms above; impending engagement, pregnancy or good luck, respectively). This site even includes alternate shapes like a frog, binoculars and a slice of cheese, which ought to throw anybody for a loop.

KEEPSAKES		

800-878-2446 — PearlRiver.com

This "first Chinese American department store" has been offering quality merchandise since before the US allowed trade with modern China, so you can imagine how good the store is now that the doors of international commerce are open. It's an excellent place to find a variety of authentic Asian products, including many for your wedding and reception. Highlights include gorgeous paper lanterns and parasols that are, if anything, even more beautiful. A wonderful place to shop regardless of your family's traditions.

FAVORS & DECOR		

PerfectDetails.com   650-576-4927

Seeking to play a role in "defining your style," this simple, visually oriented site serves a simple purpose: accessorizing the bride. Different parts of the body are highlighted, with sections devoted to gloves, shoes, wraps, garters, tiaras and other headwear. Each item is terrifically luxurious, and appropriately expensive, and all sections feature bizarre little quotes like, "Tiaras flirt with the eye." Peculiarly aggressive, it may be just what you need to get things done.

| APPAREL | ATTENDANTS | BRIDE |
| JEWELRY | SHOES & ACCESSORIES | STATIONERY |

PetalGarden.com   866-878-5770

Flower petals can paint a wedding with vibrant color in almost every conceivable place, whether they're being tossed through the air, sprinkled across a table or thrown onto the ground. Of course, cleaning up fresh petals can be a trying task, especially when they stain. The petals offered by this site skirt that issue. Freeze-dried and silk rose petals comprise pretty much the entire selection, but there are so many colors available you may want to spend a couple of hours deciding just how many and which variety. There are few better ways to expand your wedding palette.

| FLOWERS | | |

PeterFoxShoes.com   212-431-7426

The Bridal and Wedding Shoe Glossary on this designer shoe site explains such things as shantung silk, the louis heel, the blucher lacing method and dozens of other shoemaking details ranging from the interesting to the arcane. While this may be a helpful resource as you pursue the perfect bridal or bridesmaid shoes for your nuptials, more immediately useful might be the shopping categories, which feature the leather and satin boots and pumps that made Peter Fox a popular name in the footwear world.

| ATTENDANTS | BRIDE | SHOES & ACCESSORIES |

Photo.Stamps.com

310-482-5800

Back in 1992 the US Postal Service ran a consumer election to see if America wanted a commemorative Elvis Presley stamp to feature the young Elvis or a more mature King. Young Elvis won, leaving many dissatisfied. Thank goodness the technology now exists to make everybody happy. Whether you want to order a book of stamps featuring the older Elvis, or, more appropriately, wish to commemorate the bride and groom, this innovative postal site allows you to design your own valid stamps featuring any image you desire (within a published set of content restrictions). This almost makes personalized address labels seem silly.

STATIONERY		

PictureItPostage.com

800-576-3279

It's one of the marvels of modern technology that even something so official as a postage stamp may be custom-made to include your own picture. Once you've selected the perfect invitations and announcements to match your shared sense of style, veer on over to this specialty site to upload a picture of the happy couple, and post them with panache. The cost may exceed that of regular stamps, but it will ultimately be cheaper than adding a photo to your stationery.

STATIONERY		

PlumParty.com

800-227-0314

If we were to choose any web site to party with, it would probably be this one, and it's not just because of the terrific invitations that would go out, or the fantastic decorations we could expect. These guys offer everything but the actual life of the party, ranging from serving trays and table settings to party favors. Some may be suitable for your wedding reception, but more likely this stuff will be perfect for a bridal shower or bachelorette party.

FAVORS & DECOR	PARTIES	STATIONERY

PlusSizeBridal.com   866-757-274

Claiming to be the "only on-line bridal store catering exclusively to the plus-siz
bride," at the very least this very well-stocked special-occasion dress shop migh
be the only place she needs to visit. The seemingly endless selection of brid
gowns, bridesmaid dresses, flower girl dresses and mother-of-the-bride dresse
covers enough stylish ground to satisfy most tastes, and an efficient, flexibl
customer service policy will ensure the picky bride finds the best-fitting choic
available, all at a reasonable price.

APPAREL SHOES & ACCESSORIES	ATTENDANTS	BRIDE

PrincessBrideTiaras.com   513-554-197

This Cincinnati-based boutique is particularly devoted to those elegant accessorie
that make brides the most beautiful women in the world. Of course, it begins wit
a stunning assortment of elegant and affordable tiaras. Large enough to warra
various categories, this might be the greatest assemblage of tiaras and bridal ha
accessories online, and you could easily get so wrapped up you fail to notice th
gorgeous bridal jewelry, gloves, wraps and veils; so be sure to pay attention.

BRIDE	JEWELRY	SHOES & ACCESSORIES

PrintIcon.com   866-774-684

This site is a frustrating collision of flash and substance. The animated layout
these pages looks cool, but between new browser windows popping up all ov
the place and dedicated submenus at every turn, it's really quite a hassle. On th
other hand, we wouldn't be talking about the site at all if its wares weren't wor
looking at, and these paper designs are astounding, incorporating very desirabl
colors and patterns for printing, including several metallic and transluce
varieties for do-it-yourself invites, and plenty of envelopes and card stock fo
thank-you cards. Tough to love, but hard to ignore.

DIY	STATIONERY	

888-373-7437   # ProFlowers.com

Promising flowers "direct from the grower," this online florist pretty much has it all: international shipping, same-day delivery, exotic plants and fruity gift baskets. They also offer several different ways to shop, including Shop By Occasion, which should make it fairly simple for you to find bouquets and boutonnieres. There's no need to restrict yourself to the Weddings category, though, as any number of the vibrant available arrangements would make a lovely centerpiece.

BRIDE GROOM	FAVORS & DECOR SHOES & ACCESSORIES	FLOWERS

877-237-3773   # Prom-Dresses.com

When a girl starts scouring the earth for a prom dress, almost nothing will do, and even this site devoted to special-occasion gowns might let her down. But send that same girl to this same site in search of bridesmaid dresses and a funny thing happens: all the dresses suddenly look fantastic! The shop's single focus allows you to browse dozens of pages of dresses in a quest to avoid the dread pastel ruffles of bridesmaid lore and, happily, most of the apparel you'll see treads a fine line between prim and sexy.

APPAREL	ATTENDANTS	

949-675-6404   # PulpFactory.com

If you've got a color printer, a color or style in mind and want to mail out your invitations right away, this site offers customizable invitation, note card, greeting card and label designs that allow you to print from your own computer, ultimately saving you a great amount of time, effort and money. If you don't have a color printer, you can still play, going through the same automated selection and layout process, and simply asking the site to do the work for you. Basically, their job is to make it run smoother and easier for the customer; the way it should be.

DIY	STATIONERY	

PulpInvitations.com   800-371-179

We love to see companies create something unique, especially in such a cluttere
field as invitations. This online stationer may not offer much, but the invites
announcements and enclosures you'll find here stand out, with interesting us
of ribbon, vellum and the occasional spiral bindings. Of course, if you think th
shop's invitations are great, wait until you get a load of the programs, such as th
fanning design that will elegantly cool your guests as it tells them what time th
reception starts.

STATIONERY

RedEnvelope.com   877-733-368

Whether they be celebratory, obligatory, romantic or condolent, Red Envelop
lives up to its promise to furnish "gifts for all occasions." Shopping by Occasion
you'll find items earmarked for every attendant. However, you might as we
shop for particular recipients, because most items on this large site may b
personalized, and just about every single one makes for a useful, thoughtful an
entertaining gift.

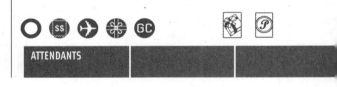

ATTENDANTS

RibbonShop.com   877-742-514

One perk of internet retail is the opportunity to specialize in a product so specific
only a global market could really justify your store's existence. This Illinois we
shop has been successful for years, strictly selling "bolts of beautiful, high
quality American-made ribbons." Just when you think it's hard to get excite
about ribbons, a glance at these pages shows you just how exhaustive a selectio
you can put together if you really try. Whether you want ribbons for your flora
arrangements, invitations or favor boxes, this one's got you covered.

FAVORS & DECOR   STATIONERY

800-459-1025   Roamans.com

Having spent the last sixty years outfitting the plus-size woman, this store's claim to offer "fashion, fit and value" has some merit. Aside from the advertised sizes 12W-44W, the site also offers petite and tall sizes, with a selection covering everything from denim and leather apparel to outerwear, sleepwear, swimwear, formalwear, career attire and lingerie. Of course, it's the formalwear that you'll want to pay special attention to, especially if you're shopping with the mother of the bride.

APPAREL	ATTENDANTS	

206-679-0289   RomanticFlowers.com

If you want to make sure to imbue a sense of romance in your wedding decor, take a good look at this do-it-yourself site, which eschews modern trends for decidedly classical tastes, usually involving floral patterns. Much of it has to do with favor packaging, ribbons, silk petals and plenty of craft supplies, with plenty of tips on creating your own flower arrangements. You'll also find some handy party supplies, including hanging lanterns and napkins. Sentimental patterns abound.

DIY	FAVORS & DECOR	

972-769-8432   RomanticHeadlines.com

In terms of bridal apparel, this homegrown site offers everything but the dress, the fact of which may not be lost on the groom. Established by the Jenkinses, a Dallas couple intent on showing off both his web design prowess and her homemade headpieces, this simple shop has expanded to include everything from jewelry on down to lingerie, hosiery and shoes, as well as some accessories for both ceremony and reception. Whether or not each product is an original Jenkins design or pieced together from other collections becomes unimportant, as it's all pretty nice, and hardly ever boring.

| APPAREL | ATTENDANTS | BRIDE |
| JEWELRY | KEEPSAKES | SHOES & ACCESSORIES |

Ross-Simons.com 800-835-1343

An almost impossibly large assortment of trinkets and collectible gifts fills the pages of this site, which may be easier to use if you request the company's catalog and strictly order online to expedite the process. Figurines, crystal, ceramics, ornaments and collector's plates; you will find hundreds of these items, and that's just in the Gifts section. Table Accessories opens the selection to an even wider variety, though all pretty much of the same taste. Essentially, there's nothing terribly exciting or awe-inducing here, but nothing that bad either.

ATTENDANTS	JEWELRY	KEEPSAKES

RubyEtViolette.com 877-353-9099

If the thought of soft, chewy cookies loaded with chocolate chunks makes your mouth water, wait until you get a load of this homegrown cookie specialist's site. The cookies here are just as we've described, only they also include additional items such as dried fruit, ginger, pistachios, marshmallows, toffee and caramel. You could gain thirty pounds just imagining the fifty-two possibilities, but we're recommending the site anyway, as they've thought to include beautiful favor packaging options.

FAVORS & DECOR	FOOD	

RustyZipper.com 503-233-2259

There aren't many stores where you can find leisure suits, disco shirts, Hawaiian shirts and 80s-style windbreakers all in one place. This is just such a store. Featuring one of the best vintage apparel selections available anywhere, it's no surprise to find a swinging selection of suits and tuxedos from eras past. Arranged by decade, clothing article, size and price range, browsing through these clothes is a breeze, and finding memorable garb for the groom and his men assured.

APPAREL	GROOM	

SaveTheDateStickers.com
888-272-5111

The specialty of this singular stationer's site is written right into its name: save-the-date stickers. The shop's save-the-date cards are cute and contemporary, but don't otherwise stand out from other selections except for the fact they include a sticker reminder for your guest to post on their calendars. And if some of your invited guests don't keep calendars? Opt instead for the magnetic kits (assemble yourself) so they can put that helpful little reminder on their refrigerators.

DIY	STATIONERY	

ScotYard.com
800-636-0116

We wouldn't have thought it, but this site proves you only have to go as far as Kentucky in search of authentic Scottish garb for your Celtic wedding. Of course you'll find kilts aplenty, along with a wealth of other tartan apparel, in particular a formalwear section that allows you to put together an incredible suit to purchase or rent. There are also some pretty outstanding wedding bands, the occasional sporran and bagpipes, complete with a book of traditional wedding songs.

APPAREL GROOM	ATTENDANTS JEWELRY	BRIDE SHOES & ACCESSORIES

ShoeBuy.com
888-200-8414

With hundreds of name brands and thousands of products, what more could you want from this, "The World's Largest Site for Shoes?" How about free shipping and returns? Yes, the massive shoe shop makes great strides to provide strong customer service—but how are the shoes? Well, considering they offer footwear for every member of the wedding party—even the bride—we're going to say you'll want for nothing as long as you know everybody's sizes.

ATTENDANTS SHOES & ACCESSORIES	BRIDE	GROOM

ShopForWeddings.com   800-725-6763

The name makes little real-world sense, but this is a "Wedding Superstore," with the "guaranteed lowest prices," so we'll give them a little credit. Actually, all manner of trousseaux and wedding gifts fill these assorted pages. From centerpieces to favors and even those little wedding-themed disposable cameras that inspire certain guests toward bursts of newfound creativity (move aside, Annie Leibovitz!), this site has just about every little thing you need to throw a wedding in the right direction.

| ATTENDANTS | BRIDE | FAVORS & DECOR |
| JEWELRY | PARTIES | STATIONERY |

ShopLoveMe.com   818-707-3003

This site is brought us by the combined efforts of an event planner and invitation/decor designer from good old Los Angeles, California. Popular with celebrities and fashion magazines alike, the two have conspired to deliver a thoughtful assortment of luxe gifts and hip party accoutrements, granting us all access to the graceful backdrops of a Beverly Hills wedding or Hollywood cocktail party; and given that the scenery is often the most important and enduring part of such events, this makes it among the best available in the world.

| ATTENDANTS | FAVORS & DECOR | KEEPSAKES |

SimplyElegantGowns.com   845-469-5062

Including A-line, empire and ball-gown styles, these wedding dresses are indeed simple and elegant, whether a size 4 or size 20. Only minor details distinguish these classic gowns, which means that despite a fairly minimal selection, any woman on the hunt for a design of uncomplicated beauty stands a good chance of finding something perfect, and at prices that are likewise not outrageous. A similar but color-imbued sensibility can be found in the Bridesmaids section, and all can be topped off by matching varieties of veils and tiaras, for prim, traditional perfection.

| APPAREL | ATTENDANTS | BRIDE |
| SHOES & ACCESSORIES | | |

510-381-4731   SophiesFavors.com

Getting together with your bridesmaids to assemble favor boxes, attach tags and tie ribbons can be a fun way to distract yourself from prewedding jitters. If you have the spare time in the days leading up to the big day, this site offers adorable favors and packaging components for you to put together. While your hands are busy you can use the time to wax nostalgic, gossip or dream about the future, and perhaps wonder why you didn't talk the boys into wrapping the favors.

DIY	FAVORS & DECOR	

800-306-8070   SparklersOnline.com

Nothing brings your wedding to life quite like a bit of fire, in this case in the form of wedding sparklers. Clearly, this isn't a great idea if your wedding is held in a barn or the Southern California wilderness during the dry season, but, as the site illustrates, in a safe environment sparklers can make for an exciting photo op. If you would like a little bit of bang, the site also offers tiny champagne-bottle-shaped poppers, named for the popping sound they make when they shoot silver streamers into the air. These are less dangerous, but more messy.

FAVORS & DECOR		

203-853-4774   StClairIceCream.com

According to this site, "molded, hand-crafted frozen desserts graced the tables of royalty for centuries," but the practice has waned in the modern era, presumably due to the relative lack of monarchs. Fortunately, this Connecticut-based specialty ice cream and sorbet shop was founded "to carry on the artisanal tradition." It does so magnificently, offering delicious, single-serving desserts in marvelous flower, swan, heart, fruit and bell shapes, among others. These treats are sure to delight your guests.

FOOD		

StylishChoice.com   800-454-0017

As charming as it is small, this family-owned-and-operated business out of Massachusetts features a smattering of lovely bridal accessories, including headpieces, jewelry and garters. But the real reasons to visit the site are the bridal handbags and shoes. Available in dyeable satin as well as black and metallic colors, these pumps, sandals, purses and clutches are beautiful as-is, and only get better when you add on one of the braided, floral and beaded appliqués.

| ATTENDANTS | BRIDE | SHOES & ACCESSORIES |

SuitYourself.com   203-255-8889

Refined gentlemen and fashionable blokes alike will appreciate this men's clothier that offers a wonderful selection of smart-fitting suits, sport coats, overcoats and tuxedos. These aren't your bargain-basement, generic-cut jacket-and-trouser combinations, and the distinction shows. Single- and double-breasted designs are available by fine labels like Baroni, Belvest and Ermenegildo Zegna, among others, to make for the best-dressed groom and groomsmen you've ever seen.

| APPAREL | GROOM | |

SurroundingsFlowers.com   800-567-7007

For floral arrangements that are at once simple, elegant and extraordinary in their beauty, trust the slim selection offered here to win you over quickly and often. Whereas many florists will offer more variety, they'll usually overcomplicate things. On the flipside, these bouquets are content to minimalize, showing utter confidence that tightly bundled calla lilies, or a single orchid spike can express more beauty and sentiment than the most elaborate arrangement. When Surrounding Flowers does add an element of variety, they tend toward understated combinations that blend similar colors that will take your baby's breath away.

| FLOWERS | | |

800-554-0924   **Teuscher-NewYork.com**

As extravagant as candies get, the chocolates of this New York store actually hail from Switzerland, meaning they're pedigreed, and have come a long way to please your taste buds. However, if the boxed confections or elegantly wrapped truffle favors aren't posh enough for you, never fear; the Fantasy Packaging section of the shop proves as enticing as it sounds, with candies gorgeously packaged in floral arrangements or made to resemble animals. Top of the list, though, have to be the candies packaged to resemble the bride and groom; as cake toppers, these will probably taste better than the cake.

FAVORS & DECOR		

800-390-9784   **TheKnot.com**

Perhaps better as an all-in-one wedding resource than an online shop, this large site offers a little bit of everything for your wedding, including invitations, custom postage, decorations, attendant gifts and keepsakes, and even offering the occasional personalization option. However much you like it as a shop, there's little doubt the wedding planner software, local service guides, gown research tool and registry will come in handy as your big day approaches.

ATTENDANTS STATIONERY	FAVORS & DECOR	KEEPSAKES

586-293-4744   **ThePerfectPear.com**

Dressing the most precious young members of your wedding party calls for an exceptional kind of shop, and lucky we are to have found this one. With flower girl and junior bridesmaids dresses topping a lovely selection of children's special-occasion attire, this Michigan store's devotion to every age and size makes it well worth a visit, whether you're outfitting infants or teens. The ring bearer suits and tuxedos only add to the appeal. You can only hope the groomsmen will look so dapper.

APPAREL	ATTENDANTS	

ThePerfectToast.com   866-500-2036

When the feeling is right but words won't come easy, the inarticulate speaker will be happy to have this site's special service available. A staff of speechwriters will custom-package your history and sentiments into eloquent elegance, with the occasional punch line so they don't fall asleep in the back rows. The Instant Toast option takes ready-made speeches and inserts the names of the bride and groom, whereas a Custom Wedding Toast will actually incorporate your own anecdotes and as much or little of your personality as good taste demands.

ATTENDANTS	GROOM	

TheWeddingLibrary.com   212-327-0100

While this site may not be as comprehensive as the New York City boutique that spawned it, we can only hope it will grow over time as the selection of bridal accessories we found here leaves us wanting more. For the moment, though, we'll just have to be satisfied with the few precious shoes, handbags and headpieces currently available, and maybe plan a trip to the Big Apple location which promises to offer the world's "most talented, in-demand, creative and hard to find suppliers."

ATTENDANTS	BRIDE	DOCUMENT
SHOES & ACCESSORIES		

ThingsRemembered.com   866-902-443

What began as a small key-making shop in Ohio has transformed over the course of several decades to become "the nation's leading and most experienced retailer of personalized gifts." A surprisingly huge assortment of products are available for personalized embroidering, engraving or embossing. The site's set up to shop by occasion or recipient, but if you use the Advanced Search you should easily find specific products like pens, flasks, watches, barware, lighters and jewelry for your attendants.

ATTENDANTS		

800-216-7107   ThompsonCigar.com

Cigars make for a fine groomsman or father-in-law gift wherever you buy them, provided you shop with good taste. This Key West, Florida, tobacconist offers plenty in the way of fine smokes, but the best part about their service is the personalization option. You may either add your own text to the cigar band or upload your own logo design. In either case you'll receive a beautiful box filled with personalized premium cigars, rolled with the Dominican-grown house blend. Of course, if the bride doesn't condone a celebratory, post-dinner reception smoke, this favor should probably be confined to the bachelor party.

ATTENDANTS	GROOM	

800-843-3269   Tiffany.com

There's no more famous jewelry store in the world and, if you like a sure thing, it's a pretty safe bet that somebody receiving a gift in a trademark Tiffany's blue box will be thrilled. Of course, that's because an internationally esteemed selection of merchandise goes along with the name recognition, incorporating the finest diamonds, most sterling silvers and other high-grade metals and stones into beautiful designs, whether engagement rings or napkin rings. We fancy the wedding bands and attendant gifts, and you can bet we're not alone.

ATTENDANTS JEWELRY	BRIDE	GROOM

212-645-6890   TinaTang.com

Hollywood couldn't tell a better story. Tina Tang turned her back a Wall Street career (with Goldman Sachs, no less) to follow her dream of becoming a jewelry designer. Now this daring spirit has been captured in her collection of chokers, necklaces, bracelets and earrings. She uses handpicked crystal, glass, pearls and semiprecious stones to find a sort of cosmic harmony in her designs, and whether she expresses this with bold colors or elegant silverwork, her "bliss" shines through, for the bride and her retinue.

ATTENDANTS	BRIDE	JEWELRY

TK-Designs.com   877-293-249

This site's exceedingly difficult to use, but even tougher to leave out, given i
remarkable assortment of wedding apparel for men and women. The Africa
& Ethnic Collection in particular features garments rarely seen in wedding we
shops, but in truth, the entire bridal and bridesmaid selection includes uniqu
dresses and gowns. The good news is, they'll make these clothes according to yo
own measurements. The bad news is, recording and entering these measuremen
might prove too complicated for the average American shopper, almost makir
this a do-it-yourself enterprise.

APPAREL GROOM	ATTENDANTS	BRIDE

TogetherBook.com   800-472-171

Once the fine times of your big day have passed, you might want to consid
commemorating them with the help of this innovative site. A Together Book
essentially a photo album; however, your photographs are actually bound in
the album to create a lasting and memorable document. Other options incluc
custom-stamping your names onto the front, and adding a custom slipcover
preserve your pictures with even more panache.

KEEPSAKES		

TopsMalibu.com   808-828-007

The unique party favors offered by this small site "should spark conversatio
create surprise, awaken creativity, and allow for a dose of silliness." Primaril
this will be accomplished with the Bami, or "Surprize" Balls that, when unwrappe
reveal a continuing string of trinkets and confetti cones. There are plenty of oth
original favors that will help your seated guests bond over dinner, and sparkle
that everyone will enjoy after dessert.

FAVORS & DECOR		

404-685-9818   TurqBridal.com

Long gone are the days when bridal jewelry spanned only two choices: diamonds or pearls. Take a look at this site and you may decide that your wedding attire could use a splash of color after all. While plenty of dazzling traditional options may warrant the bulk of your attention, a beautiful assortment of semiprecious necklaces give you a moment to reconsider. At the very least you may find the perfect bridesmaid gift among these baubles; they may even be enough to make up for the dresses!

ATTENDANTS	BRIDE	JEWELRY

888-968-4889   TuxedosOnline.com

It's not hard to guess this site's specialty, nor is it hard to shop here. Once you know your rudimentary measurements, browsing the various Classic, Contemporary, Colored, Designer, White and Cutaway tuxedos is a simple matter, and each may be ordered with a variety of options, including cummerbunds, vests, cufflinks, spats, top hats and suspenders. A $100 Tuxedos category may prove particularly alluring to those on a tight budget, but you may also find an incredible deal in the Used Tuxedos section. Do it right the first time and you should never need to shop here again.

APPAREL SHOES & ACCESSORIES	GROOM	JEWELRY

888-455-0222   TweetyTunes.com

If you like the idea of hiring a singer/songwriter to compose a song especially for your big day, take a look at the service offered by this rather interesting site. Simply enter the your names, fill out a short questionnaire about yourselves (how you met, what are your interests, etc.) and a professional musician will compose and record a song to order, which you may play at your ceremony or reception. The key in using this service is to reign in your expectations: it won't be a number-one hit, but it might bring a bit or sweetness or levity to your party, depending on how you answer those questions.

KEEPSAKES		

UltimateWedding.com   800-300-5587

A long engagement will leave you plenty of time to browse this "ultimate online wedding mall," which may be appropriate as, between deep clicking and varied selection, seeing every available option will take a while. This is not the site for you if you've vowed to keep it simple, but if you're willing to be tempted by the likes of personalized toasting flutes and animal cake toppers, you could be in for a lot of fun at a fair price. The site also provides a bevy of online planning tools, which will become quite necessary the more elaborate your wedding day gets.

DOCUMENT KEEPSAKES	FAVORS & DECOR SHOES & ACCESSORIES	JEWELRY STATIONERY

USA-Flowers.com   888-463-5257

Fans of FTD and Teleflora florists should greatly appreciate this site, which culls the finest arrangements of both national mainstays into one terrific selection. Whether you want centerpieces, bouquets, corsages, boutonnieres or nosegays, you'll find all the selection you could want, and arrange for them all to be delivered in a timely fashion so they'll look as fresh and smell as sweet as your big day deserves.

FLOWERS		

USPS.com   800-275-8777

First class, postcard, water-activated, self-adhesive, rolls, books, flags, liberty and commemorative: it's all about stamps, and this web store hosted by the perennial men in blue may save you a trip to the local post office. Sure, it sounds like a simple matter, but finding just the right stamps to match your invitations can be difficult in your local branch. Online, you may buy stamps in any denomination, with special selections for oversized envelopes and RSVP cards.

STATIONERY		

VeilsALaMode.com
800-880-6645

This unique specialty store out of San Francisco presents an interesting case. It actually sold its veils, tiaras and bridal hair accessories out of a small brick-and-mortar shop for more than a decade before ever selling its wares online. Eventually, this site became so prosperous that the proprietor actually shut the doors of her local business to focus exclusively on the virtual marketplace. Its history aside, this is a lovely place to look into all manner of bridal headdress; it's no wonder they've done so well.

ATTENDANTS	BRIDE	SHOES & ACCESSORIES

VeryDifferentCakes.com
323-466-1480

The difference referred to by this site's name doesn't really involve the cake, itself. Rather, it refers to the cake toppers: specifically, the Swarovski crystal cake toppers, available in heart, flower and butterfly shapes. By far the most popular, though, is the crystal monogram toppers. With all shapes and letters (& ampersands) available in a variety of colors, you'll have no trouble choosing a topper to match your wildest wedding dreams.

FAVORS & DECOR		

VictoriasSecret.com
800-970-1109

What can be said about Victoria's Secret that hasn't been said a million times before? Their ubiquitous presence has literally set a standard for modern lingerie, and their seasonal catalogs have become a cultural staple, pleasing to both men and women. Featuring some of the most beautiful women in the world, and some of the finest intimate fashions, these pages will inspire plenty of honeymoon romance, whether you stick to the Bridal section or not.

APPAREL	BRIDE	

VintageWedding.com   800-660-3640

Some people like to don multicolored spandex and recite their vows while leaping
out of a plane; some like to eke out a slightly more traditional wedding ceremony.
This shop is most definitely for the latter. Featuring gorgeous vintage gowns,
tuxedos and accessories, these items were designed in an era long since gone and
are rich in romantic appeal. In a way, even the site itself is vintage, with outmoded
web design and a difficult ordering process. But you definitely shouldn't miss it.

APPAREL	BRIDE	SHOES & ACCESSORIES

WeddingDepot.com   615-791-9529

Cut right to the basics with this wedding superstore, which delivers all the
traditional items that immediately come to mind when you plan a wedding.
Start with the stellar wedding album components, then move on through a solid
assortment of other keepsakes, including tussie-mussies, wedding cake charms,
handkerchiefs, guest books, cake servers, toasting flutes and garters. The
occasional less-common items are not to be missed, including bridal shower and
bachelorette party games, novelty bridal party apparel and bridal emergency kits
(which, truth be known, may also be useful for the groom).

DOCUMENT	FAVORS & DECOR	KEEPSAKES

WeddingFavorites.com   714-505-5799

If one goal of your reception is to impart to your guests just how fashionable you
truly are, you'll appreciate the trinkets, stationery and accents offered by this
retailer of "stylish favors for weddings and bridal showers." Some pretty original
stuff, like silver-plated fortune cookie boxes, sandalwood fans and seashell
napkin rings indicate the type of creative merchandise you might find here but
in no way represents the tone of the entire catalog. Anything you'll find here is
merely a matter of taste, except for the bride-and-groom teddy bears; they're
just for cuteness' sake.

FAVORS & DECOR	PARTIES	STATIONERY

WeddingFavors.com
651-493-0884

Strictly speaking, these guys offer more than just wedding favors; they have sections for pretty much any kind of party you can think of, from Baby Showers to Quinceañeras. But who cares? We're talkin' about weddings, and that means cakeboxes and candies, and place cards for the reception. Okay, so there's not a whole lot going on in the Wedding Favors section. But remember those other sections we were talking about? Many of them offer things that are nonspecific enough to work at a wedding. A little creativity goes a long way here, and that may be what your guests appreciate most.

| DIY | FAVORS & DECOR | STATIONERY |

WeddingFlowersAndMore.com
877-268-3683

Though not very easy to use, this site nevertheless offers a valuable assemblage of floral options for your ceremony and reception. It begins with many lovely bouquets, corsages, boutonnieres, petals and attractive table centerpieces, any of them arranged either with fresh flowers or with silk. The "More" in the site's name refers to plenty of ribbon, favor boxes, aisle runners and all the assorted hardware you'll need to put everything in place. To that end, this shop proves invaluable to the wedding do-it-yourselfer, as pretty much everything you see here can be done on a budget if you throw in a little elbow grease.

| DIY | FAVORS & DECOR | FLOWERS |

Weddingish.com
866-933-3386

This unusual bridal boutique forgoes the stuffiness often associated with weddings in favor of a lighthearted, almost rompy approach. Novelty garb including monogrammed slippers, crystal-adorned thongs and personalized aprons is doubtlessly meant more for the days leading up to the wedding than the ceremony itself, and a few modern, breezy attendant gifts, including a bevy of iced cookies, will at least please the flower girl and ring bearer. Plant your tongue firmly in your cheek before you view this one.

| APPAREL GROOM | ATTENDANTS | BRIDE |

WeddingPetals.com   706-332-4888

There's nothing quite like the hurling of confetti through the air to lend a festive atmosphere to any moment. Of course, one must eventually wonder: who's going to clean all this up? This site proposes a more ecologically sensitive alternative in the form of flower petals and herbs. They call it Petalfetti, "For Fairy Tale Endings," and it may sound silly to say, but it's sure aromatic. Stowed in paper cones or glassine envelopes, the rose petals, rosemary and lavender make for elegant missiles as bride and groom embark upon their new married life.

FAVORS & DECOR	FLOWERS	

WeddingRings.com   800-522-1175

The most important accessories for the bride and groom are the ones they're not wearing when the ceremony begins. This ring specialist offers a fine selection of unique, designer and handmade wedding bands to dress your fingers with the sort of elegance true love inspires. Of course, during any visit to this site, you ladies won't be able to ignore the dazzling assortment of gold and platinum engagement rings also available....

BRIDE	GROOM	JEWELRY

WeddingSolutions.com   800-606-9200

For the most part, this site should be used as a planning resource, as it's well equipped to guide you through the ins and outs of preparation, etiquette and decoration, and even to connect you with honeymoon and registry assistance. However, as the product of four wedding retailers joining forces, it's not surprising that the Shopping pages turn out to be many. To a greater or lesser degree, most of your ceremony and reception needs may be met within these pages, ranging from aisle runners and wedding bubbles to favor boxes and marriage certificates. Nothing particularly stands out, but everything is appropriate.

DOCUMENT STATIONERY	FAVORS & DECOR	KEEPSAKES

888-338-8818   **WeddingThings.com**

This site says, "our team of buyers shop the world to bring you the newest and most elegant essentials for your big day." The results can take all day to view, running the gamut from personalized favors to bridal accessories, with a few novelty items thrown in for fun. With plenty of tried-and-true decorative styles and the occasional something different, this weddings superstore can be a good place to start, or a reliable last stop.

BRIDE SHOES & ACCESSORIES	DOCUMENT	FAVORS & DECOR

408-396-1365   **WeddingTulle.com**

Because having too many options is never a problem for the picky bride, we refer you to this small but worthwhile seller of invitations, place cards and favor packaging. There's not a lot of merchandise here, in fact there's very little, and yet somehow it seems capable of satisfying a wide range of customers. If every online retailer were this efficient, in terms of style, this book would be a lot shorter. A beacon of hope for the exasperated wedding planner, don't visit this one first, or its charm will be lost on you.

FAVORS & DECOR	FLOWERS	STATIONERY

419-609-0450   **WendyKromer.com**

For some beautiful wedding favors that add a touch of sweetness to the celebration, check out these fantastic decorated cookies. It's a very limited selection, found by following the Online Store link. Some cookies take the shape of wedding cakes; others, engagement rings or hearts. Or, you can opt for monogrammed cookies, decorated in either pink or blue to represent the bride and groom. You'll need to order these well in advance, but they'll probably be eaten by the time the main course is served.

FAVORS & DECOR	FOOD	

WesternWeddings.com 888-273-7039

Perhaps the only bridal-related site to feature a section called Wedding Hats, it's pretty obvious what sort of clientele this shop is here to serve. Men shopping here take the least amount of risk by far, as the cowboy-influenced formal gear surpasses nearly every other tux you could find in terms of style, and that's not even including the boots. Women's gowns and accessories seem dazzlingly beautiful for the hardworking frontier woman, but given that this is internet shopping, most tastes can be better suited elsewhere, and should be. Good shopping for the few and rugged among us.

| APPAREL | ATTENDANTS | BRIDE |
| FAVORS & DECOR | GROOM | SHOES & ACCESSORIES |

WhiteCrushWedding.com 800-306-8738

The top of a wedding cake attracts a surprising amount of attention, and we're not talking about frosting. There are plenty of sites in this book that offer the classic bride-and-groom topper, and even a few that take a more whimsical approach. For elegant adornments, though, it's tough to beat this specialist, which features gold, silver, crystal and stainless-steel letters for a monogrammed topper that becomes elevated to keepsake.

| FAVORS & DECOR | KEEPSAKES | |

WholesaleTableLinens.com 866-827-4177

Regardless of your reception's theme or style, this great specialty site is certain to offer table linens, napkins and chair covers to match. Selections include round, square, rectangular and oval tablecloths, including fitted and elastic options covering a wide range of textures and colors, including dozens of elegant, contemporary and whimsical patterns. Couples on a budget may even prefer to buy fabric by the yard and cut it to your own specifications, with samples available to ensure you pick exactly the right one.

| DIY | FAVORS & DECOR | |

888-494-6376 — WindsorFashions.com

Contemporary fashions meet budget considerations with this family-run shop that caters to the modest girl with glamorous aspirations. With a variety of current styles on display for very reasonable prices, a bridesmaid's best bets will be found, appropriately enough, in the Bridal Collection area of the site. The registry feature allows you to coordinate with your bridesmaid wherever she may reside, at which point you may debate which of the many available colors will look best on her.

| APPAREL | ATTENDANTS | |

877-557-5675 — WonderfulGraffitiWedding.com

An intriguing idea spawned this unique specialty site: create vinyl stickers that will adhere to most surfaces and spell out a message to your wedding guests. In other words, you can create your own signs to put on the doors to a church or on the back window of the bride and groom's getaway car. The personalized messages are available in a wide variety of colors and are not backed by any adhesive solution, so they won't damage any surface. It's not exactly traditional, yet. You'll have to see it to believe it.

| FAVORS & DECOR | | |

800-316-2083 — WrappedHersheys.com

Putting a candy-wrapper twist on a classic, this unique specialty site offers tasty and memorable favors in the form of Hershey's chocolate bars. The trick is this: the wrappers are custom-printed with your text and/or photos. So, you may commemorate the happiest day of your life in a dessert, or send out the sweetest engagement announcement your friends will ever likely receive. Just be wary of melting chocolate in the summer months.

| FAVORS & DECOR | FOOD | |

WrapSmart.com   888-269-9727

The concept of a wedding favor is open to interpretation, but there's little doubt that presentation counts for something. Whether you're packaging cookies, candies, candles, petit fours or Matchbox cars, the favor boxes and other packaging offered by this wrapping supply specialist should give you plenty of options when it comes to matching your decorative scheme, and adds a little mystery to what exactly the favor is.

DIY	FAVORS & DECOR	STATIONERY

Zappos.com   888-492-7767

The "web's most popular shoe store" offers every type of shoe imaginable, and of course this includes plenty of options for your entire wedding party. Of course, men's and children's dress shoes abound, but more remarkable are the hundred-plus bridal shoes. Browse by heel height and style, and the discriminating bride is sure to find footwear to match her budget as well as her gown. One visit will probably make you a fan for the rest of your marriage.

ATTENDANTS SHOES & ACCESSORIES	BRIDE	GROOM

Zazzle.com   800-980-9890

When it comes to things like t-shirts, posters, note cards and postage stamps, our choices have always been limited by the visions of those people who go into such businesses. Thanks to this site, we no longer have to wear shirts advertising another designer, send the thank-you cards bearing another's pleasing illustration or mail a stamp commemorating somebody else's hero. Here you may custom design your own products, uploading image files from your computer to take control of your products, whether they're wedding favors or special gifts.

ATTENDANTS	FAVORS & DECOR	

866-942-6663   **Ziamond.com**

Diamonds may be a girl's best friend, but in truth that has mostly to do with a century's worth of clever marketing. For all the luster of diamond jewelry without the exorbitant pricing, take a good look at this cubic zirconium specialist. Available in gold, silver and platinum settings, the engagement rings here are as beautiful as any other stones you'll find. Granted, if you're a stickler on that one point, you can always just use this shop to find some cost-appropriate bridal jewelry. Only a jeweler can tell the difference.

BRIDE	JEWELRY	

312-404-5080   **ZoeOliver.com**

There is plenty of jewelry out there that would smartly adorn your attendants, however, if you'd like to peruse a simply beautiful set of baubles in enough colors to match just about any hue of bridesmaid dress, take a look at this designer's "spiritual" wares. Your girls will love the actual thank-you gift as well as the gesture, and you'll rest secure in the knowledge that they'll be perfectly accessorized as they stand to support you on the big day. Everybody wins.

ATTENDANTS	JEWELRY	

212-579-9824   **ZubieNYC.com**

You enter the colorful world of semiprecious jewels when you log on to this relatively simple-to-use designer-baubles site, and no matter which hue you prefer you should be satisfied. Shop for earrings, necklaces and bracelets and you'll find selections sorted by color and price range. There aren't enough brooches to warrant such categorization, but some of these one-of-a-kind pieces prove memorable indeed. However you choose to browse, it will be hard to find something you dislike among the lovely assortment of chunky trinkets.

ATTENDANTS	BRIDE	JEWELRY

Bridal Registries

This section of the book will lead you to some of the most fun on-line shopping ever: the kind you don't have to pay for. It may seem a little greedy, but it's a time-honored tradition that your wedding guests will contribute to your new life together by giving you all those things you need to set up house. Of course, these aren't merely gifts—these are gifts you pick out for yourself!

Not only has internet shopping been embraced as a way to shop from bridal registries, it has dramatically improved the ease and availability of registered products to generous guests. Your loved ones can shop for you from anywhere in the world and have the gift sent directly to your home, all within a few minutes. You won't have to haul forty pounds worth of china and flatware home from your reception, and you may update and change the registered items as you go. In other words, online shopping is the greatest thing to happen to weddings since the invention of crab puffs.

While buying your gifts will be easy for family and friends, choosing the right products with which to begin your life together may be a little more difficult; not because the browsing process will necessarily be difficult, but because there are a lot of fine online registries to be considered.

As proof we offer more than one hundred excellent registries, any of which may cater to your personal tastes and needs, and your guest list's budgets. Here you will find every style of traditional registry, whether your style is sleek and modern or cozy country French.

The best way to get started is to decide which sort of gifts you might actually use. If you are not formal dinner party people, skip the crystal and fine china. If you have no need for a melon baller or salad tosser, perhaps a kitchen and housewares shop isn't where you want to go. The registry system originated as a means of outfitting a young household, with a bride often moving straight from her parents' home into domestic bliss.

But these days, it's much more common for couples to already live together before getting married, and quite unlikely that the bride doesn't already have a perfectly suitable collection of dinnerware and linens, thank you very much. Consequently, nowadays it's acceptable to register for just about anything, including camping equipment, artwork and even home electronics equipment. One type of registry that's grown tremendously in popularity lets guests contribute to your honeymoon, while others will actually collect toward paying down your mortgage.

✳ UNDERSTANDING THE ICONS

ART & ENTERTAINMENT

Though it verges on decor, original artwork has become a popular registry item in its own right, whether in painting or sculpture form. We also found some first-edition books that lovers of literature will covet.

BARBECUE

Though a grooms may not be overwhelmingly enthusiastic about new dinnerware and kitchen appliances, the idea of a new grill and associated accessories might just get him excited about the registry process.

BARWARE

Entertaining doesn't always need to involve dinnner, so when you register for service-ware, consider building a bar with mixing tools, glassware, decanters and bar furniture.

BED & BATH

Now that you'll be sharing a bedroom (officially) you might want to get new bedding—just remember, your husband will be happier to help make it if he likes it too. Use a similar compromise when registering for towels.

CHARITY

Even if you have plenty of stuff and want no more, your guests will feel more comfortable giving you something. Deflect the generosity by having them give donations in your name to a charity you value.

CLEANING & STORAGE

It's not terribly exciting, but picking up a few functional housewares will help make keeping your newly outfitted home a lot easier. As it happens, there are some pretty nice looking mops and brooms out there.

ECO-FRIENDLY

Whether you've long been an advocate of environmental sustainability, or have only recently gained an awareness, you may register to fill your home with eco-friendly housewares, bedding, power supplies, decor and more.

ELECTRONICS

Registering for a plasma screen might be asking for a lot, but supplementing your home entertainment needs through a registry might just seem like a good idea to your most generous friends and family.

FURNISHINGS

Furniture, accents and other decor turn up at a lot of online registries, so you'll have ample styles from which to choose. Always remember, you can send guests to a couple of different places.

HONEYMOON

One of the most exciting advances in bridal registries has to be the advent of the honeymoon registry. Especially for couples with well-stocked homes, this option gives you the financial flexibility to go further for longer.

KITCHEN & APPLIANCES

Make more of your long future of meals together by registering for new cookware, cutlery, kitchen gadgets and small appliances. There's definitely a lot out there to choose from.

PATIO & GARDEN

There's nothing saying your domestic registry has to be restricted to the inside of your home. Whether it's patio furniture, landscaping gear or tools, accents and plants for your garden, your life outside only gets better.

SPORTS & OUTDOORS

If your life in the outdoors veers toward the more rigorous or adventurous side, you may want to consider registering for camping equipment and other active and athletic gear.

TABLEWARE

Last but not least, fine china, casual dinnerware and other serving supplies probably comprise the most popular registry items, and are most commonly featured in these shops. *Bon appetit!*

✳ BRIDAL REGISTRY TIPS

REGISTER EARLY

Regardless what you choose, register early so people can start purchasing gifts as soon as your engagement party, and so you'll have plenty of time to write thank-you notes as the gifts come in.

BUYER (AND RECIPIENT) BEWARE

Even though it's not your dime, make yourself familiar with a site's exchange and return policies, and in the case of honeymoon and cash registries, whether the registry service charges a fee to the gifter or giftee.

HOLD YOUR GIFTS

Some shops will agree to hold your gifts, either shipping the products on command, or all at once (which may cut down on shipping costs). Investigate this option, and be aware they should still notify you as gifts are purchased so you may send thank-you notes as you go.

✳ REGISTRY SERVICES

The following sites offer unique or all-encompassing registry services, which you may consider in the unlikely event the hundred we've assembled don't address your full range of needs:

Felicite.com

MyGiftList.com

MyRegistry.com

TheKnot.com

WeddingChannel.com

TheBigDay.com

❊ REGISTRY ITEMS

Since it can be a bit overwhelming to think of all the items you may wish to register for, we have put together a handy checklist of the basics. Here is our registry cheat sheet:

Kitchen Tools

- ◎ Cookware
- ◎ Can opener
- ◎ Canister set
- ◎ Corkscrew
- ◎ Cutting board
- ◎ Grater
- ◎ Ice cream scoop
- ◎ Kitchen shears
- ◎ Knife block
- ◎ Knives (chef's)
- ◎ Knives (steak)
- ◎ Measuring cups/spoons
- ◎ Mixing bowls
- ◎ Pizza cutter
- ◎ Salt and pepper mills
- ◎ Sharpener
- ◎ Slotted spoons
- ◎ Spatulas
- ◎ Whisk
- ◎ Wooden spoons

Cookware

- ◎ Baking pans
- ◎ Pyrex ware
- ◎ Roaster and rack
- ◎ Saucepan
- ◎ Sauté pan
- ◎ Skillet/frying pan
- ◎ Stockpot

Kitchen Appliances

- ◎ Bakeware
- ◎ Blender
- ◎ Bread machine
- ◎ Coffee grinder
- ◎ Coffee maker
- ◎ Cookie sheets
- ◎ Crock Pot
- ◎ Espresso machine
- ◎ Food processor
- ◎ Ice cream/yogurt maker
- ◎ Juicer
- ◎ Microwave oven
- ◎ Mixer
- ◎ Rice cooker
- ◎ Sandwich press
- ◎ Steamer
- ◎ Teapot
- ◎ Toaster
- ◎ Waffle maker
- ◎ Warming tray

Barware
- ◎ Champagne flutes
- ◎ Cocktail mixer
- ◎ Decanter
- ◎ Double old fashioned
- ◎ Highball/tumblers
- ◎ Ice bucket/tongs
- ◎ Martini glasses
- ◎ Shot glasses
- ◎ Stemware
- ◎ Water goblets

Place Settings
- ◎ Bowls
- ◎ Bread-and-butter plates
- ◎ Coffee cups
- ◎ Dessert plates
- ◎ Dinner plates
- ◎ Glassware
- ◎ Salad plates
- ◎ Saucers

Flatware
- ◎ Cake knife
- ◎ Dinner forks
- ◎ Fish forks
- ◎ Fish knives
- ◎ Hostess set
- ◎ Dinner knives
- ◎ Salad forks
- ◎ Soup spoons
- ◎ Teaspoons

Table Settings
- ◎ Butter dish
- ◎ Chargers
- ◎ Cloth napkins
- ◎ Creamer
- ◎ Gravy boat
- ◎ Napkin rings
- ◎ Place mats
- ◎ Serving bowls
- ◎ Serving platters
- ◎ Sugar bowl
- ◎ Tablecloth

Bed & Bath
- ◎ Bath mat
- ◎ Bath sheets
- ◎ Bath towels
- ◎ Bathroom scale
- ◎ Comforter
- ◎ Duvet
- ◎ Guest towels
- ◎ Hand towels
- ◎ Pillows
- ◎ Shams
- ◎ Sheets/pillow cases
- ◎ Shower curtain
- ◎ Wash cloths

NOTES:

_____

_____

_____

_____

_____

_____

_____

_____

_____

_____

_____

_____

_____

_____

_____

_____

_____

_____

_____

_____

AgentProvocateur.com   44-0-870-727-4169

Granted, this steamy London lingerie site isn't a registry you'll notify your grandparents about, but for a bridal shower registry, there's no harm in having your girls outfitting you for the sexiest honeymoon on record.

AHappyPlanet.com   888-424-2779

Just when you thought you were going to have a tough time filling your home with all-organic, earth-friendly products, this site offers "sustainable, quality products which do not compromise labor, animals or the earth."

Alibris.com   877-254-2747

Book-lovers with fully furnished homes should consider registering with this massive specialty bookstore. Filled with first editions, signed copies and other rarities, you can build a prestigious library to share for eternity.

Amazon.com   800-201-7575

The first name in internet retail has come a long way from its origins as strictly a bookseller, as evidenced by its wedding registry, which features such a broad spectrum of products our iconography can't do them justice. You'll like it.

APerfectWeddingGift.com   760-451-8677

Registries are an opportunity to fill your home with new things, but if you have nice things and would rather have a home to fill, or need help covering your wedding costs, this registry takes the awkwardness out of asking guests for cash.

BallardDesigns.com   800-367-2775

Shop founder Helen Ballard Weeks has literally won awards for keeping a tasteful home, so it's no surprise that this furniture, accents and service-ware retailer offers a classically tasteful selection.

800-954-3004 — BDJeffries.com

This small but charming shop seems to have fashioned a lifestyle out of its beginnings as a crocodile and alligator accessories brand, but now you may also procure some great barware, china, home decor and the occasional antique.

800-462-3966 — BedBathAndBeyond.com

With its vast selection of contemporary home furnishings, small appliances, bedding, barware and serving items, this popular housewares chain makes the perfect registry for the modest and tasteful.

888-774-2424 — BergdorfGoodman.com

Crystal decanters, anaconda skin placemats and Fabergé desk clocks tell the story: this high-end Fifth Avenue department store is richly tasteful, verging on the exotic. A dream registry.

713-665-0500 — Berings.com

Whether it's barware, blenders, china or vacuum cleaners, this Texas retailer has a knack for finding household objects that somehow look classy, egalitarian and cool all at once. Not to be missed.

800-606-6969 — BHPhotoVideo.com

That this site offers video and camera equipment, you may have guessed, but there' also a lot of quality audio and home theater gear. Will your wedding guests gladly stock your entertainment needs? There's only one way to find out.

800-777-0000 — Bloomingdales.com

The classic department store chain delivers all the quality and selection that made it a household name before the days of e-commerce; only now its registry is convenient for your family and friends regardless of where they live.

BoDanica.com   800-654-4674

This San Diego area housewares retailer offers a small but surprisingly diverse range of dinnerware, flatware, and stemware, including handcrafted dinnerware from French, Italian and American brands.

BombayCo.com   800-829-7789

British Colonial styles are represented by this unassembled-furniture specialist, which happens to count lovely selections of preassembled tableware, bedding and table linens among its offerings.

Borsheims.com   800-642-4438

Look under Gifts to find this site's very upscale selection of barware and tableware, then fervently hope you have friends and family who can support your lavish entertaining needs and desires.

CampingWorld.com   866-601-2323

Traditionally, couples register for household items to outfit their home. However, if your wedded bliss involves the endless exploration of American highways, register here to turn your recreational vehicle into a roaming dream home.

CeramicaDirect.com   800-270-0900

Everything on this site is beautiful and easy, which is a credit to its national origins: Italy. A love of Majolica is the best reason to register here, as its selection is unparalleled.

ChefsCatalog.com   800-884-2433

If you find pots and pans beautiful, dig this site's broad range of cooking tools kitchen gadgets and electrics, and help keep your kitchen up to par with you interior decoration.

ChefsResource.com
866-765-2433

You don't need to have a huge kitchen to register here, but you'll want one. Aside from a massive selection of chef's tools and appliances, you'll find excellent grilling options and affordable tableware. Good eating awaits.

Chiasso.com
800-654-3570

Chiásso (the Italian word meaning "uproar") promises "inspired design for the home," and though its breathtaking furniture, accents, bedding and entertaining pieces don't always cover the basics, it doesn't disappoint.

Comfort1st.com
443-539-1440

This site seems to be a comfort specialist, but turns out to be an everything-under-the-sun megastore. You will still find plenty of comfortable products, they're just alongside appliances, cleaning tools, grills and camping gear.

Cooking.com
800-663-8810

If anything's missing from this everything-kitchen site, only the most experienced chef will notice. For the rest, the cookware selection is supreme, and the grills, barware, dinnerware and cleaning supplies making the registry that much better.

CooksCorner.com
800-236-2433

Domestic life seems all the more appetizing when you register with this cooking specialist. Every traditional countertop appliances may be had, as well as a few more exotic machines.

CountryDoor.com
800-341-9477

This specialty furniture and housewares retailer offers "unique products that reflect a love of traditions and celebrate the family," but your guests may require special instructions to find your wish list on this site.

CrateBarrel.com   800-967-6696

This slick and modern housewares chain has quickly become one of the most popular registries of the young urban couple, propagating its subtle elegance nationwide. It rarely disappoints.

CrystalClassics.com   800-999-065?

When only the best serving pieces will do, turn to this impressively stocked crystal and fine china retailer, which houses brands such as Waterford, Kosta Boda, Orrefors, Swarovski and Wedgwood.

CurranOnline.com   800-555-665?

The great dining, living room and patio furniture on this site ships from the manufacturer, meaning you get a great price on this stuff—rather, your wedding guests do. How excited do you think they'll be about the free freight shipping?

Cutlery.com   800-859-699?

You're unlikely to find a more professional selection of cutlery anywhere other than on this cookware specialty site, which offers plenty of excellent pans, appliances and gadgets.

DesignPublic.com   800-506-654?

Designer bedding, wallpaper and lamps head up a selection punctuated by hip barstools and coffee tables with this San Francisco-based modern housewares shop that encourages "personalizing your space."

Dillards.com   800-345-527?

This oft forgotten department store makes itself memorable with massive selections of china, bedding, barware and more. Finding items bride and groom agree upon should prove easy; choosing which to register may prove hard.

800-348-3872   DiversDirect.com

If your life together's going to begin below sea level, you may want to register with this scuba and snorkeling specialist. It's unconventional, but let them know it's going toward your aquatic honeymoon, and your guests might pitch in.

800-944-2233   DWR.com

This San Francisco-based seller of upscale European furniture offers what may be the best online selection of designer furniture we've seen, and it can all be yours, provided your wedding guests can afford it.

626-969-3707   EcoChoices.com

The clear emphasis of this site is to promote the fact that living an ecologically sustainable lifestyle is a choice we can make as consumers; and rarely are environmentally sound products so rewarding as when they're registered.

212-251-0621   eTableTop.com

Founded on the principle that "tableware doesn't need to be expensive or fancy," this site delivers a unique assortment of lovely, modern service-wares that run the gamut from inexpensive to moderately inexpensive.

323-655-1908   Fitzsu.com

Not many shops will make the effort to offer beautiful toilet brushes, but that's just the kind of store this is. Nontraditional design enthusiasts will get a huge kick out of just about everything in this unique home store.

800-367-8866   Fortunoff.com

This Brooklyn housewares shop constantly expands its selection to outfit your home with updated takes on classic styles. You'll find everything from fine china to barbecue grills, all of it tasteful and refined.

Frontgate.com 888-263-9850

Though not exactly comprehensive, there's no doubt this purveyor of high-end "lifestyle accessories," features products of exceptional taste; basically the kind of stuff everybody has but better, particularly when it comes to entertaining.

Gaiam.com 877-989-6321

Proving that sustainable living is not just a fad, the excellently designed shop offers items as aesthetically pleasing as they are functional, which almost takes the fun out of curbing your reliance on chemicals and plastics.

GarnetHill.com 800-870-3513

You'll find lamps, rugs, towels and other household items on this catalog site, but the best selection is its sheets, comforters, quilts and any other term you can come up with for a blanket. However, this wish list must be emailed.

GiveFun.com 888-448-3386

A different kind of registry is offered by this site; rather, several different kinds. Your guests actually buy you gift certificates, which may be redeemed to pay for your honeymoon travel, or for use at a variety of popular retailers.

GraciousStyle.com 888-828-7170

This purveyor of bed and table linens has the goal to "inspire discerning clients to create the perfect settings for celebrating a life of luxury, elegance and sophistication." Some lovely dinnerware and flatware may also be found.

GreenFeet.com 888-562-8873

We're getting used to seeing the eco-lifestyle represented online, but every time we visit this site we're surprised at just how deep its variety of environmentally friendly products is. An excellent, globally responsible registry.

877-344-8453 — Guild.com

This "source of the finest artists and their work" has a great selection of original, contemporary art pieces. The great thing is, this stuff isn't limited to paintings, but includes gorgeous tableware and home accents.

800-882-8055 — Gumps.com

Founded in San Francisco on the heels of the Gold Rush, this store once serviced the newly rich, which explains the high quality of its wares. Particularly appealing is the dinnerware and bedding, but everything is definitely top shelf.

425-332-3732 — HeathCeramics.com

Delighting in "simple and authentic" beauty, this tableware specialist offers a very small but breathtaking assortment of classic yet contemporary place settings, the likes of which you won't find anywhere else. Don't miss it.

800-430-3376 — HomeDepot.com

If one of these behemoth home-improvement stores are near you, prepare to revel in the massive and surprisingly diverse products you may register for here, including exercise equipment, appliances and grilling gear.

800-809-5862 — HoneyLuna.com

This honeymoon registry itemizes different components of your trip—airfare, lodging, tours, rental car, etc.—and presents them to your guests in a traditional format, allowing them to feel comfortable paying for your dream vacation.

858-433-1506 — HoneymoonWishes.com

Registering for your honeymoon allows your guests to feel like they've contributed to your fun, whether it be in the form of a special tour, room service, suite upgrade or in-room massage. All of these are more fun to give than place settings.

HSN.com   800-933-2887

That's right, the Home Shopping Network has moved beyond your television screen and onto your computer, with a massive selection in tow. You may register here for just about anything; no remote control necessary.

IDoFoundation.org   202-466-5922

At the top of this site's charitable registry options is a service allowing you to collect donations for your favorite cause. It already features many national nonprofits, but once registered, you may request to add one close to your hearts.

InternationalVilla.com   800-759-9696

This family-owned retailer out of Colorado offers a wealth of fine china, crystal, silverware and barware. Finding anything isn't always easy, but with plenty of terrific brands to choose from, odds are good you'll find something you like.

JCPenney.com   800-322-1189

It's quite possible this popular department store was your parents' bridal registry. The quality of merchandise holds steady today, though we can assure you it has been updated, so you won't wind up with your mom's bedding and appliances.

JustGive.org   866-587-8448

Making it easy to locate a cause you favor, this online network of over 800,000 charities aims to make the donation process efficient and satisfying, for you and your guests.

Kohls.com   866-887-8884

This growing department store chain offers a great selection of mid-market items at fair prices, outfitting your home with the sort of housewares that have all but become traditional through decades of ubiquity.

LavenderFieldsOnline.com
866-898-5461

"Located in the historic coastal hamlet of Port Jefferson, New York," this shop brings its quaint, small-town atmosphere to the web, with a lovely assortment of country chic blankets and home accents.

LaylaGrayce.com
801-474-1990

This shop sort of adheres to family-friendly styles, which means a betrothed couple may find plenty of bedding to outfit their loving home, whether children are already in the picture, or fondly anticipated.

LeeValley.com
800-267-8735

If home improvement is on your married agenda, try registering with this enormous online hardware, woodworking and garden supply store. You can stock up on both the raw materials and the tools you'll need to build a happy home.

LekkerHome.com
877-753-5537

The great thing about this "Unique Home Furnishings" site is that it delivers what it promises; we doubt there's anything in this shop's unusual selection that you already own, and you may wind up wanting a lot of it.

LnT.com
866-568-7378

This national retailer urges you to "dream big, pay little," which is something for your wedding guests to appreciate while you're appreciating the wide assortment of contemporary housewares.

Macys.com
800-289-6229

Everything you'd expect to find in a department store is just the beginning of what you get here, and with massive selections of dinnerware to bolster terrific bedding, kitchen tools, appliances and decor, this registry won't let you down.

Magellans.com   800-962-4943

Prepare for your honeymoon with this unique registry, which will outfit your travels whether you're going to the jungle or to the beach. Travel accessories, appliances, comfort aids and clothing will get you there in style and ease.

ManorHG.com   866-406-2667

The definition of fine china has loosened a little bit over the years, and rarely will you find better modern takes on special-occasion dinnerware than on this high-end site. Definitely a registry you want your rich relatives to see.

MaxwellSilverNY.com   212-799-1711

The beautiful confluence of modern styles found here may be attributed to the two-dozen high-end New York brands and boutiques represented by this stellar site. It should be no trouble for savvy urbanites to find their preferred tastes.

MichaelCFina.com   800-289-3462

Extensive dinnerware, flatware, glassware and barware selections make this ultra-high-end gift and housewares catalog a must-see. Any kitchen accoutrements you find are just icing on the cake.

MixedGreens.com   866-647-3367

Though this modern online dealer features only a limited number of artists, each of them offers fashionable and aesthetically appealing original work representative of contemporary times, and may turn out to be a sound investment.

MontroseTravel.com   800-666-8767

This all-in-one travel operator offers an easy way to register your honeymoon. All you do is book your dream escape, including travel, lodging and activities, then send your guests to a personal web site to contribute.

866-888-6677

MossOnline.com

The virtual rendition of one of the most intriguing concept retail stores in the nation, this site features a wealth of deliriously hip home accents, cookware, tableware and furniture.

866-458-8687

MusiciansStorehouse.com

The best kind of toys are available on this musical instrument site. Register here and you may fill your newly wedded home with music. Remember, though, you'll owe your guests a recital sometime down the line.

800-443-0339

Nambe.com

This popular line of modern serving accoutrements will keep your kitchen and bar gleaming with beautiful crystal, porcelain and polished metal products. This is definitely not your parents' registry.

888-888-4757

NeimanMarcus.com

With enough designer wares to furnish a year's worth of magazines, in and outside the home, this site is a virtual playground for those with rich tastes; register here if you're absolutely hungry for the good stuff.

800-270-6511

NotNeutral.com

If your life's too fun for stuffy, formal service-ware, check out this small line of funky and alluring dinnerware, barware and table linens. You won't find anything else like it, which is a shame because it's too cool to miss.

800-600-9817

Organize.com

This site is an obsessive-compulsive's dream come true, with myriad storage and organization products that might happen to fit nicely into your decorative scheme, even if they happen to be trash bins or laundry hampers.

Pier1.com   800-245-4595

"Filled with unique, quality merchandise from over 50 countries," this ever-updating catalog somehow straddles the line between luxurious and practical, satisfying those with eclectic tastes.

PlaceSettings.com   704-847-6773

Exquisite china, stemware, flatware and crystal bar pieces are available from this often difficult site. Lines like Wedgwood, Waterford, Spode, Lennox, Reed & Barton and Royal Worcester make it worthwhile.

PotteryBarn.com   888-779-5176

Combining classic American styles with influences from the world over, the Pottery Barn's exclusive line of products offers sturdy simplicity and reasonable prices, and has been a popular registry destination for years.

REI.com   800-426-4840

If you'd rather regster to outfit your home away from home, use this outdoor sporting goods specialist to register for camping, climbing, hiking and winter gear.

RestorationHardware.com   800-762-1005

The intriguing combination of modern and retro style offered by this burgeoning chain makes it a terrific registry for those who desire a classic household, including cleaning tools that are actually nice looking.

RetroModern.com   877-724-0093

Both vintage and new perceptions of modern furniture, accents and service-ware are on keen display on this site that wants to encourage a deeper understanding of and appreciation for 20th-century design. For those of adventurous taste.

800-835-1343   **Ross-Simons.com**

Though maintaining a strong focus in silver, crystal and porcelain collectibles, the Ross-Simons catalog has expanded considerably to include a fine array of jewelry, housewares and dinnerware, making for a great bridal registry.

800-631-2526   **RudisPottery.com**

Brands like Reed & Barton, Waterford and Wedgwood are only the beginning at this tableware specialty site. Penty of fine china, stemware and flatware may be found; it just might take awhile. It'll be easy for your guests though.

800-554-6367   **SchweitzerLinen.com**

For those of us who demand that only the finest of fineries should come into contact with our persons, this Manhattan-based luxury retailer offers a dazzling array of bedding, table linens, towels and more.

800-223-3717   **ScullyAndScully.com**

Learn what the denizens of Park Avenue, Manhattan, have known for seventy years: this upscale department store offers one of the finest registries in the country. Fine china, lovely everyday dinnerware, crystal and silver abound.

800-262-3134   **SilverQueen.com**

Though it offers one of the best selections of fine china, sterling-silver flatware and opulent crystal, registering on this horrendously difficult site will test your patience at every turn. Fortunately, your guests should find it easier to use.

800-426-3057   **SilverSuperStore.com**

Though on the surface it seems like a flatware specialist, the truth is this massive site's china selection is just as huge. Consequently, it may take time to find perfection, but odds are good it's here.

SoftSurroundings.com   800-240-7076

The world is tough enough without abrasive bed linens. At least, that seems to be the premise behind this site, which specializes in the sort of soothing products especially favored by women, but easily appreciated by sensitive men.

Spiegel.com   800-527-1577

Although you must email registry items to your friends and family (rather than have them search for your registry on the site), this Chicago department store's selection of bedding and decor might make it worthwhile.

StacksAndStacks.com   800-761-5222

Offering "homeware… for your storage and organizational needs," this site is full of crates, carts, boxes, cabinets, shelves and racks but, more surprisingly, it's loaded with appliances, furnishings and outdoor decor.

StitchChicago.com   773-782-1570

A Chicago boutique with a definite flair for the modern, the web site we found here isn't very well stocked, however, each bedding set, furniture piece, and tabletop accessory seems close to perfect, in a futuristic sense.

SurLaTable.com   866-328-5412

Boasting "over 13,500 items from more than 900 vendors worldwide," this burgeoning national retailer aims to be "a reliable source for top quality cookware and kitchen tools." Do they succeed? Boy howdy.

TabulaTua.com   888-535-6590

A fine selection of upscale service sets and accessories awaits you here; beautiful stuff to dress your table, without being so fine you must lock it away for special occasions. In other words, just right.

800-591-3869   **Target.com**

We probably don't need to decribe the vast selection available from any Target store, other than to say it's fun, contemporary and includes everything under the sun. Most of all, though, it's affordable.

888-838-5551   **TGW.com**

With a selection that seemingly never ends, this all-golf retailer might prove to be every groom's favorite registry, but this is not to say golf-loving brides won't enjoy it; after all, the Women's sections are equally well-stocked.

800-304-1141   **TheBigDay.com**

Staff travel advisors will help you put together a travel package for your dream honeymoon but, regardless, this site will help pay for the trip by hosting a registry where your friends and family can donate toward your romantic journey.

888-796-7772   **TheHoneymoon.com**

This honeymoon service allows your guests to contribute to various aspects of your travel, wherever you go and however you book it. Set up your registry, and the site will gather contributions, sending you a check in the mail.

510-549-2282   **TheMagazine.info**

Presenting distinctive designs that often feel straight out of a sci-fi flick, this furniture shop offers nothing less than a glimpse into our near-distant future. Lucky are those who register here.

888-935-5277   **TheWellAppointedHouse.com**

As you may be able to tell by the name of this site, its offerings tend to veer toward the upscale, including a surprising amount of trash bins, which, if you think about it, do play very important roles in keeping your house well appointed.

TravelersJoy.com   888-878-5569

Book your honeymoon how and where you like, then build a registry page on this handy site, which will show your guests descriptions, pictures and even videos about what they're paying for, before collecting their gifts for you.

Tupperware.com   800-366-3800

Granted, you don't want Tupperware to constitute your entire registry, but mix the handy kitchen containers with the cutlery and cookware here, and you'll be off to a good start.

UncommonGoods.com   888-365-0056

Barware, bizarreware, garden and home furnishing products may be found at this atypical housewares retailer. You might find glassware with a Holstein cow decor, an umbrella-shaped lamp or a fish stapler.

UnicaHome.com   888-898-6422

Here's a fine selection of intriguing ultramodern designs that should keep things fresh whether you're entertaining or just sitting around enjoying all your stuff. Consider it one of the best registries out there.

VivaTerra.com   800-233-6011

Driven by a "dedication to living in harmony with nature," this eco-friendly lifestyle shop offers environmentally sound home and garden products, including tableware and bedding.

Wal-Mart.com   800-966-6546

You know the largest retailer in the nation; it offers extensive shopping opportunities from coast to coast, and there's just something about being able to find all of life's accoutrements under one roof that is eminently appealing.

800-606-9200   ## WeddingSolutions.com

This helpful wedding resource doesn't stop at connecting you wih local vendors or offering you fashion tips. It allows you to set up a personal honeymoon registry site, where it will collect your guests' contributions to your dream vacation.

877-812-6235   ## Williams-Sonoma.com

This granddaddy of bridal registries is better than ever, with a web site offering everything you'd expect from the timeless catalog, but easier to share. Still a worthy choice for any couple.

800-356-8466   ## WineEnthusiast.com

If you would like to add a wine cellar or bar to your home, this is the place to register, whether you desire beautifully constructed bar furniture, brilliant stemware sets or elegant bar accessories.

877-411-9600   ## Wrapables.com

A bright array of fresh, colorful and fun home accents heads up the selection, but every page you browse will reveal something fantastic, whether it's casually cool dinnerware or exceptionally chic bedding.

877-877-0101   ## YourWeddingRegistry.com

If none of the registries in this book have what it takes, you might turn to this site, which lets you choose items from any source, then either directs you where to buy, or makes the purchase for you.

800-358-8288   ## zGallerie.com

Hip without being pretentious, upscale without being expensive, it's little wonder Z Gallerie stores have popped up across the nation over the past twenty-five years. Great for those who love to entertain.

NOTES:

_____

_____

_____

_____

_____

_____

_____

_____

_____

_____

_____

_____

_____

_____

_____

_____

_____

_____

_____

_____

NOTES:

_____
_____
_____
_____
_____
_____
_____
_____
_____
_____
_____
_____
_____
_____
_____
_____
_____
_____
_____

product index

a

accessories
see: bouquets, boutonnieres, bridesmaid, corsages, cufflinks, gloves, groom, hair accessories, handbags, handkerchiefs, hats, headpieces, jewelry, shawls & wraps, shoes, tiaras, veils

apparel
see: bridal gowns, bridesmaid, flower girl, mother-of-the-bride, novelty apparel, ring bearer, shawls & wraps, suits, ties, tuxedos

b

NOTES:

_____

_____

_____

_____

_____

_____

_____

_____

_____

_____

_____

_____

_____

_____

_____

_____

_____

_____

_____

bridal registries
key word index

Use this section as a quick reference guide to help you locate your
preferred registry products.

ART & ENTERTAINMENT: Original artwork, books, music or
movies.

BARBECUE: Grills and grilling accessories.

BARWARE: Cocktail shakers, bar glassware, bar furniture, ice
buckets and decanters.

BED & BATH: Bedding, pillows and towels.

CHARITY: Charitable donations.

CLEANING & STORAGE: Functional household products.

ECO-FRIENDLY: Environmentally sustainable items.

ELECTRONICS: Entertainment systems and other household
consumer electronics.

FURNISHINGS: Furniture and decorative accents.

HONEYMOON: Honeymoon and cash registries.

KITCHEN & APPLIANCE: Cooking tools and gadgets.

PATIO & GARDEN: Outdoor furnishings and gardening tools.

SPORTING GOODS: Camping and other equipment.

TABLEWARE: Dinnerware and fine china sets.

NOTES:

_____

_____

_____

_____

_____

_____

_____

_____

_____

_____

_____

_____

_____

_____

_____

_____

_____

_____

_____

_____

NOTES:

_____

_____

_____

_____

_____

_____

_____

_____

_____

_____

_____

_____

_____

_____

_____

_____

_____

_____

_____

wedding shops
key word index

Use this section as a quick reference guide to help you fidn the right wedding product selections.

APPAREL: Special occasion attire for all members of the wedding.

ATTENDANTS: Accessories, apparel and gifts for bridesmaids, groomsmen, ring bearers, flower girls and mothers of brides.

BRIDE: Accessories and apparel for the bride.

DIY: Do-it-yourself projects, ranging from printing your own invitations to baking a wedding cake.

DOCUMENT: Helpful planning, necessary paperwork and products to keep a record of the occasion.

FAVORS & DECOR: All manner of trinkets and decorative items to put the fine touches of your ceremony and reception.

FLOWERS: Florist sites, as well as those offering bouquets, corsages, boutonnieres and petals.

FOOD: Appatizers, sweet favors, baking supply and more.

GROOM: All things related to the groom, and in most cases his groomsmen as well.

JEWELRY: Wedding bands, engagement rings, bridal jewelry and lovely bridesmaid gifts.

KEEPSAKES: Traditional wedding accoutrments that you'll want to keep as mementos.

PARTIES: Products for the planning and execution of bridal showers, bachelor and bachelorette parties.

SHOES & ACCESSORIES: Accessories and footwear for all members of the wedding.

STATIONERY: Invitations, announcements, save-the-date cards, programs, thank-you cards and more..

DIY

DOCUMENT

FAVORS & DECOR

JEWELRY

Abazias.com, 69
Adin.be, 69
AdvantageBridal.com, 70
AllysonSmith.com, 71
Anandia.com, 72
AntiqueAndEstate.com, 74
AntiqueJewelryExch.com, 74
AntiqueJewelryMall.com, 74
BenSilver.com, 78
BlueNile.com, 81
BouquetJewels.com, 82
BrooksBrothers.com, 84
CatanFashions.com, 85
Costco.com, 87
Cufflinks.com, 87
Emitations.com, 93
eWeddingAccessories.com, 94
eWeddingShoes.com, 94
ExclusivelyWeddings.com, 94
Festivale.net, 97
GaraDanielle.com, 101
HairComesTheBride.com, 104
HawaiianWeddingShop.com, 105
JoannSmyth.com, 111

Longmire.co.uk, 115
MichaelCFina.com, 174
MikaWed.com, 117
MikiMotoAmerica.com, 117
ModelBride.com, 118
Mondera.com, 119
MyGlassSlipper.com, 122
Nordstrom.com, 124
PaulFredrick.com, 129
PerfectDetails.com, 130
PrincessBrideTiaras.com, 132
RomanticHeadlines.com, 135
ScotYard.com, 137
ShopForWeddings.com, 138
Tiffany.com, 143
TinaTang.com, 143
TurqBridal.com, 145
TuxedosOnline.com, 145
UltimateWedding.com, 146
WeddingRings.com, 150
Ziamond.com, 155
ZoeOliver.com, 155
ZubieNYC.com, 155

KEEPSAKES

AdvantageBridal.com, 70
Beau-Coup.com, 77
CatanFashions.com, 85
ClassyBride.com, 87
DaisyArts.com, 88
DavenportHouse.com, 89
DavidsBridalGifts.com, 89
EscapeConcepts.com, 93
ExclusivelyWeddings.com, 94
FancyFlours.com, 95
FavorAffair.com, 96
FavorsEtc.com, 97
FByS.com, 97
FiligreeMonograms.com, 98

GiftSongs.com, 101
HouseOfBrides.com, 106
MoonRockPaper.com, 120
MyJeanM.com, 122
PeachTreeCircle.com, 129
RomanticHeadlines.com, 135
ShopLoveMe.com, 138
TheKnot.com, 141
TogetherBook.com, 144
TweetyTunes.com, 145
UltimateWedding.com, 146
WeddingDepot.com, 148
WeddingSolutions.com, 150
WhiteCrushWedding.com, 152

PARTIES

Bachelorette.com, 75
BachelorettePartyShop.com, 76
BacheloretteSuperstore.com, 76
Beau-Coup.com, 77
BellaRegalo.com, 77
EscapeConcepts.com, 93

FavorsByLisa.com, 96
JRCigars.com, 112
PlumParty.com, 131
ShopForWeddings.com, 138
WeddingFavorites.com, 148

SHOES & ACCESSORIES

AdvantageBridal.com, 70
BenSilver.com, 78
BestBridalPrices.com, 79
BlueFly.com, 81
BlueTuxshoes.com, 82
BridalPeople.com, 83
BridalShoes.com, 83
BrooksBrothers.com, 84
CatanFashions.com, 85
CattleKate.com, 85

ChinaBridal.com, 86
ClassyBride.com, 87
DyeableShoeStore.com, 91
eWeddingAccessories.com, 94
eWeddingShoes.com, 94
ExclusivelyWeddings.com, 94
FByS.com, 97
Festivale.net, 97
FiligreeMonograms.com, 98
HairComesTheBride.com, 104

SHOES & ACCESSORIES (CONT.)

STATIONERY

NOTES:

_____
_____
_____
_____
_____
_____
_____
_____
_____
_____
_____
_____
_____
_____
_____
_____
_____
_____
_____

NOTES:

_____

_____

_____

_____

_____

_____

_____

_____

_____

_____

_____

_____

_____

_____

_____

_____

_____

_____

_____

_____

NOTES:

_____
_____
_____
_____
_____
_____
_____
_____
_____
_____
_____
_____
_____
_____
_____
_____
_____
_____
_____
_____
_____

company index

NOTES:

_____
_____
_____
_____
_____
_____
_____
_____
_____
_____
_____
_____
_____
_____
_____
_____
_____
_____
_____
_____

NOTES:

_____
_____
_____
_____
_____
_____
_____
_____
_____
_____
_____
_____
_____
_____
_____
_____
_____
_____
_____
_____
_____

NOTES:

_____
_____
_____
_____
_____
_____
_____
_____
_____
_____
_____
_____
_____
_____
_____
_____
_____
_____
_____
_____
_____